A Computational Model
of First Language Acquisition

World Scientific Series in Computer Science

Published

Forthcoming

Series in Computer Science — Vol. 20

A COMPUTATIONAL MODEL OF FIRST LANGUAGE ACQUISITION

Nobuo Satake
Department of Information Science
Faculty of Science
University of Tokyo
Japan

World Scientific
Singapore • New Jersey • London • Hong Kong

Published by

World Scientific Publishing Co. Pte. Ltd.,
P O Box 128, Farrer Road, Singapore 9128
USA office: 687 Hartwell Street, Teaneck, NJ 07666
UK office: 73 Lynton Mead, Totteridge, London N20 8DH

**A COMPUTATIONAL MODEL OF
FIRST LANGUAGE ACQUISITION**

ISBN 981-02-0139-7

Printed in Singapore by Utopia Press.

Preface

This monograph is a revised version of my 1988 doctoral dissertation, "First Language Acquisition as Problem Solving: Learning of the Correct Application of Rules through Overgeneralizations," completed at the University of Tokyo, under the supervision of Professor Yamada-Hisao.

Our study in this monograph focuses mainly on the topic "what sort of innate knowledge enables children to acquire first language." The approach is computational. We have built a computational model, named BUD (*B*ring *U*p a *D*aughter), on the basis of the data linguists and psychologists have collected. We shall try to answer this question by describing BUD.

There is a long-running dispute between nativists and empiricists regarding first language acquisition. BUD is based on the empiricists' view. There are two phenomena which can be considered as evidence supporting this view. First, children make a number of rules, in acquiring a first language, which can be seen in a pivot structure in the two word stage and a phrase structure in the later stage. Second, overgeneralizations can be found in the acquisition of every aspect of a language. Once children form a rule or a principle, they tend to apply it to cases to which it should be not applied. Thus, they are positive learners of languages they first meet. First language acquisition can be regarded as learning the correct application of a number of rules through overgeneralizations.

BUD has no built-in knowledge of language structures, but has a built-in procedure by which it computes the structure of a given language. BUD learns the correct application of rules concurrently in its databases, and accounts for overgeneralizations of rules as the results of interactions among rule-learning processes. BUD deals with such interactions with its category-formation/integration/disruption mechanism. On the basis of this mechanism, some predictions can be made regarding hidden parts in the four-stage progression in learning the past tense forms of English verbs.

A number of people are to be thanked for making this monograph possible.

I would first like to express my gratitude to Professor Yamada-Hisao, my supervisor, for his patience and invaluable suggestions in the course of this research. He inspired the work reported herein, and his guidance and valuable advice encouraged me in completing it.

I would also like to express my gratitude to Professor Eiichi Goto, who made arrangements for polishing my English, and proposed publishing this monograph.

I am deeply indebted to Mr. Yoshihiko Ono for all his assistance and helpful comments. He introduced me to the program facilities, and taught me how to prepare the documents on various computers.

I am specially thankful to Mr. Noriyuki Murata and Mr. Satoshi Matsuoka who improved the computing environment, enabling me to make good progress in implementing BUD and writing documents.

I am very grateful to my colleagues of Yamada Laboratory for their many helpful comments.

Finally, I would like to thank Mr. Douglas R. Dawson in F. J. Kurdyra and Associates co., ltd. for polishing my English.

October 1989   Nobuo Satake

Table of Contents

CHAPTER 1

INTRODUCTION

1.1. Motivation

The central aim of our study is to find something which is common to all languages. Our previous study (Satake 1986, Satake and Yamada 1987) on a transfer approach in translating natural language expressions including metaphors was motivated by the problem that the pivot in machine translation might be impossible for metaphorical expressions which may have several interpretations. The pivot is an ideal semantic representation which includes information on context. On the other hand, the present study on a mechanism for first language acquisition is motivated by a marvel of babies as language learners. They can be regarded as neutral language learners, because they can acquire any languages spoken around them. Furthermore, they learn languages they first meet more completely than adults learn second languages. It is especially difficult for us to acquire a sense of grammaticalness for grammatically complex expressions. Thus, our study in this monograph focuses on two topics:

- What sort of innate knowledge enables children to acquire first language?

- How do children and adults differ? That is, on what points do first language acquisition and second language acquisition differ?

The first topic will be discussed in several chapters, and the second topic will be discussed in the last chapter.

1.2. Two Flows for Studies of Language Acquisition

There is a long-running dispute among linguists and psychologists regarding first language acquisition. Almost all of them agree that humans are born with some innate knowledge for language acquisition. However, they are divided in their opinions about what kind of knowledge this is. Basically, they are divided into two groups. One group, traditionally called the nativist group, insists that it is linguistic knowledge itself, such as Chomsky's (1980, 1986b, 1987) universal grammar or that based on Bickerton's (1981, 1984) bioprogram hypothesis. The other group, traditionally called the empiricist group, insists that it is a procedure for computing the structure of the language a child first meets. The empiricist group can be divided into two subgroups. One subgroup, including Piaget (in Piatelli-Palmarini 1980), insists that the procedure is generally available for acquisition of all cognitive competence, and that it is like a general problem solver. The other subgroup insists that the procedure is specific to language acquisition, like LMC (the *Language-Making Capacity*) of Slobin (1985). We are developing and implementing a first-language-acquisition model named **BUD**. BUD is an acronym for *Bring Up a Daughter*. BUD is a model which computes the structure of a given language by a built-in, or innate, procedure. This monograph does not discuss the problem with regard to whether the procedure is specific to language acquisition or a general procedure which is available for acquisition of any cognitive competence. Two nativist theories are explained below in detail.

Chomsky's Universal Grammar

First, we explain the reason why Chomsky asserts that a child has abundant innate linguistic knowledge. The data a child uses as a clue for learning his native language is of very bad quality. This data comprises utterances spoken around him, and utterances addressed to him by adults. Adults often produce utterances with some hesitation, and sometimes leave them unfinished. Thus, these utterances contain syntactic errors. Nevertheless, a child completely acquires the grammar of his native language, even though no philologist has completely written the grammars of some languages. Furthermore, a child finishes acquiring his native language between the ages of four and five years. Chomsky considers that a child learns his native language too efficiently. Therefore, he claims that a child has abundant innate linguistic knowledge, and that such knowledge must be universal, because a child can learn any language spoken around him without difficulty. He calls such universal linguistic knowledge a universal grammar.

This universal grammar is a system comprising several principles which control the application of rules or determine the adequacy of representations. It has variable parts, called parameters, which can be fixed by a relatively small number of sentences belonging to a particular language. A grammar whose parameters are fixed is called a core grammar. Characteristics peculiar to a particular grammar are added to the core grammar, and thus, the particular grammar is established. If a child learned his native language based on this scenario, he would certainly acquire it in a short period.

Bickerton's Bioprogram Hypothesis

Bickerton considers that the following three questions should be integrated into one, that is, their answers should be the same:

• What are the origins of the creoles?

• How do children acquire their native languages?

• How did human languages begin?

Sugimoto (1985) explains pidgins and creoles as follows. Assume that two groups who do not have any native language in common come in contact with each other for some particular purpose, and that they need to communicate with each other. Then, a limited language system called a pidgin is born. A pidgin in the initial stage contains an extremely small vocabulary in which the majority of words are borrowed from the native language of the stronger group. Its grammatical structure is very simple. Hence, it can only handle a restricted range of topics. It is so unstable that it vanishes when the two groups break off contact with each other. For example, Korean Bamboo English was born of contact between American soldiers and Koreans in the Korean Peninsula during the Korean War, and vanished when the American soldiers evacuated the Korean Peninsula. On the other hand, when contact between two groups lasts for a long time, a pidgin comes to be used for a variety of purposes and in daily life. Children of the next generation, who grow up hearing such a pidgin, learn it as their native language. The language they use is called a creole. The difference between pidgins and creoles does not come from the complexity of the language system but from what the native languages of the speakers are.

Bickerton uses the term "creole" in a more restricted way. First, a creole comes from a pidgin which precedes it, but the pidgin must exist for less than two generations. Thus, the language born from Tok Pisin, which is a pidgin English of Papua New Guinea, and which has existed together with the indigenous language for several generations before being learned as a native language, is excluded. Second, a creole must be born in a situation where the native language of 20% of the population at most is a prior language, and where the native languages of the remaining 80% are diverse. Thus, Réunion Creole, also known as Neo-Melanesian, which was born in a situation where the native language of near half of the population had been French for twenty or thirty years since the immigration began, is excluded.

Bickerton claims that significant similarity beyond a chance level can be found among creoles which are seen in various parts of the earth in spite of their various histories of existence and linguistic backgrounds. The first generation who speak a creole grew up hearing a pidgin which was very incomplete as a language system and as an input. For their language to be adequate, they must acquire more extensive linguistic knowledge than that of their parents who speak a pidgin. Hence, Bickerton claims that they did not acquire the creole by learning it, but that they invented it. He also says that, although they also grew up hearing other languages, these languages had no influence on the creole they speak. For example, children of Japanese immigrants in Hawai became speakers of Japanese and of a creole, and the creole they spoke as well as a creole of children who did not speak Japanese was not influenced by Japanese. Therefore, Bickerton concludes that linguistic competence is genetically bioprogrammed in the human species.

1.3. Methods of Studying Language Acquisition

Traditionally, researchers study first language acquisition as follows: First, they record detailed utterances produced by particular children as the children grow up. They usually observe the children for a regular period of time every day, and record the children's utterances with the patent meanings of the utterances, and with the situations in which the utterances are produced.

For example, they record what the children are doing, and the parents' utterances addressed to the children (see Section 2.4). They generally use tape recorders, but rarely use video recorders, because the children may shrink at the sight of the video recorders.

Second, by comparing the children's utterances, they try to find common stages of acquisition (see Section 2.1) and common errors (see Section 2.2).

Third, they try to account for such common stages and common errors. Researchers can be divided into two groups according to their standpoints. Researchers such as McNeill (1970) and Smith (1973) put themselves in the adults' place, and try to account for such common stages and common errors on the basis of existing linguistic theories. They consider that children have incomplete adult linguistic competence, and regard children's language as evidence of the linguistic theories for adults. On the other hand, researchers such as Bowerman (1973) and Brown (1973) put themselves in the children's place, and try to describe and explain language development objectively. They use existing linguistic and psychological theories only as tools for explaining language development. Our model, named BUD, does not depend on any particular linguistic theories. We intend to explain language development from the standpoint of children, and not of adults.

1.4. Outline of This Monograph

Children are positive learners of languages they first meet. Once they form a rule or a principle, they tend to apply it to cases to which it should not be applied. This phenomenon is called an overgeneralization. First language acquisition can be regarded as learning the correct application of a number of rules through overgeneralizations. Although several overgeneralizations have been reported, existing models deal with them separately. BUD, a model for first language acquisition, has no built-in knowledge of language structures, but has a built-in procedure by which it computes the structure of a given language.

BUD forms a rule when it finds that two or more words have a common property. A category is defined as a set of words to which BUD applies a rule, or which BUD considers to have a common property. BUD learns the correct application of rules concurrently in its databases, and accounts for overgeneralizations of rules as the results of interactions among rule-learning processes. BUD deals with such interactions with its category-formation/integration/disruption mechanism. On the basis of this mechanism, some predictions can be made regarding hidden parts in the four-stage progression in the acquisition of the past tense forms of English verbs.

Chapter 2 explains phenomena including overgeneralizations found in language acquisition, and describes characteristics of inputs given to children. Because BUD has no built-in knowledge of language structures, it makes much of the roles played by inputs in the language acquisition.

Chapter 3 discusses what Gold's learnability theory implies about human's language acquisition.

Chapter 4 explains our position in developing BUD and its initial state. By comparing BUD and other computational models, we demonstrate characteristics of BUD.

Chapter 5 presents the whole constitution of BUD. Three modes in BUD and data flow in Learning Mode are explained here. Temporal representations and databases in BUD are briefly explained.

Chapter 6 presents BUD's category-formation/integration/disruption mechanism.

Chapter 7 describes BUD's behavior with nine sample sentences, and thus explains in detail how BUD learns the syntax of the language being learned, meanings of unknown words, inflections of words, and so on in

8

Learning Mode. The values of six parameters are also discussed here.

Chapter 8 explains data flow in Order Mode and Production Mode. How explicit negative examples work in Production Mode is exemplified here.

Chapter 9 discusses the difference between first language acquisition and second language acquisition.

CHAPTER 2

PHENOMENA IN LANGUAGE
ACQUISITION AND PRIMARY DATA

Although all children learn a first language in their own environment, they pass through similar stages of acquisition and make similar errors. Such common stages of acquisition are explained in Section 2.1, and overgeneralizations as common errors are explained in Section 2.2. Section 2.3 discusses whether or not children get negative examples in first language acquisition. Section 2.4 explains characteristics of utterances addressed to children by their mothers or other adults.

2.1. Stages during Language Acquisition

The One-Word Stage

Around the age of one year, children begin to produce words in isolation (for example, see Bloom 1973; Clark and Clark 1977). Because children talk about objects in their environment, most of these isolated words express food, toys, animals, furniture, and parts of the body. However, the role which such a word plays in a proposition which a child wants to convey can vary according to the situation. Greenfield and Smith (1976) make the following claims on the basis of their observation of two children. Initially, they produced words which expressed agents of some actions. For example, one child produced *Dada* when he heard someone enter the house. Next, they produced words which expressed recipients or patients of some actions. For example, a child produced *Ban*, when he wanted his mother to turn off the fan. Finally, they produced words which expressed possessors or positions of some objects. For example, a child produced *Lara* when looking at Lauran's bed, and *Bap* in pointing at excreta on a diaper. Children seem to be preparing for later stages where a proposition is expressed by a combination of words.

The Two-Word Stage

Around the age of one year and a half, children begin to combine two words into a sentence (for example, see Braine 1971; Brown 1973). Braine (1963) claims that a pivot structure can be found in such utterances, and that it indicates children's creativity. He classifies words which appear in two-word utterances into two groups. One group comprises a large number of words and the other comprises a small number of words. He calls words belonging to the former group open words, and those belonging to the latter group pivot words. A sentence which has a pivot structure comprises a pivot word and an open word. For example, in utterances *more page, more wet, more car*, and *more high*, *more* is a pivot word, and *page*, *wet*, *car*, and *high* are open words. In utterances *boot on, tape on*, and *fix on*, *on* is a pivot word, and *boot*, *tape*, and *fix* are open words. In general, the position of each pivot word in an utterance is determined. All open words can be uttered as one-word utterances, but some pivot words appear only in two-word utterances. Pivot structures can also be found in two-word utterances produced by children who speak Bulgarian, French, German, Japanese, Russian, and so on (Slobin 1971). Parents probably do not speak to their children in this way. Even in the two-word stage, children have the ability to form a category and a rule. This can be regarded as evidence supporting our model, named BUD.

Bowerman (1973) and Braine (1976) analyzed the roles which two words in a two-word utterance played in a proposition which a child wanted to convey. Bowerman analyzed utterances produced by a two-year-old girl named Kendole. Of utterances combining verbs and nouns, the largest number were those in which nouns played the roles of agents of actions expressed by verbs such as *Kimmy come* and *Mama read*. The second largest number were those in which nouns played the roles of patients of actions expressed by verbs such as *Look Kendole* (in the sense of looking at Kendole) and *Kimmy kick* (in the sense of kicking Kimmy). He also found a small number of sentences in which nouns played the roles of places where actions expressed by verbs occurred such as *Play bed* (in the sense of playing on the bed). Braine also found such a tendency in two-word utterances produced by children who speak English, Samoan, Finnish, Hebrew, and Swedish. It is impossible to completely express a proposition in two words. A two-word utterance lacks words which play important roles in the proposition.

The Three-Word and The Four-Word Stages

Most utterances in the three-word stage or the four-word stage consist of content words (Brown 1973). Children tend to preserve nouns, verbs, adjectives, and pronouns, but tend to omit inflections: *showed*, *goes*, and *books* become *show*, *go*, and *book*, respectively. He calls such speech telegraphic speech, because utterances which have the above tendencies resemble telegram form. For example, if the full message were "My car has broken down and I have lost my wallet; send money to me at the American Express in Paris," the telegram would be "Car broken down; wallet lost; send money American Express Paris." Three-word or four-word utterances comprising content words can express a proposition almost completely.

What is called a phrase structure can be found in such utterances (Braine 1971). The child Braine observed often expanded his previous utterances. For example, he expanded his previous utterances (1a), (2a) and (3a) into (1b), (2b) and (3b), respectively. Furthermore, he expanded (3b) into (3c).

    (1) a. Want that.

          b. Andrew want that.

          c. [Andrew [want that]].

    (2) a. Build house.

          b. Cathy build house.

          c. [Cathy [build house]].

    (3) a. Stand up.

          b. Cat stand up.

          c. Cat stand up table.

          d. [Cat [[stand up] table]].

Braine claims that such expansion indicates that the child knew that (1b), (2b), and (3c) had phrase structures (1c), (2c), and (3d), respectively. BUD forms several rules which can be translated into phrase structure rules by receiving a sequence of sentences as inputs in Learning Mode.

2.2. Overgeneralizations

Once children form a rule or a principle, they tend to apply it to cases to which it should not be applied. This phenomenon is well known as an **overgeneralization**, and indicates that children are positive learners of the languages they first meet. Overgeneralizations are not special phenomena which are rarely found in first language acquisition. Rather, first language acquisition can be regarded as learning the correct application of a number of rules through overgeneralizations. All of the following phenomena found in first language acquisition are due to overgeneralizations.

(I) Morphological Overgeneralizations

Children apply rules about suffixes of inflectional words, which they find in regular words, to irregular words. Thus, they overregularize these words. Note that they never hear these overregularized forms. In English, verbs and nouns are inflectional words.

Now we explain an example of an overgeneralization in the acquisition of past tense forms of verbs. These correct forms are acquired through the following four stages (Braine 1971; Slobin 1971; Brown 1973; Clark and Clark 1977; Fletcher 1985; Selfridge 1986; Rumelhalt and McClelland 1986, 1987):

Stage 1. Between the ages of one year and a half and two years children seldom produce past tense forms. They express both the present and the past tenses by the present tense forms.

Stage 2. Between the ages of two years and two years and a half they correctly use a small number of verbs in the past tense, e.g., *broke* and *went*. The majority of these verbs are highly frequent and irregular.[†]

[†] According to Kucera and Francis's (1967) data, the majority of high-frequency verbs are irregular. The ten highest-frequency verbs, i.e., *come, get, give, look, take, go, have, live, feel*, and *make,* include eight irregular verbs.

14

In this stage, they do not form any rules, but know a small number of past tense forms individually. Clark and Clark (1977) point out that children may not be aware that *went* is a past tense form of *go*.

Stage 3. Between the ages of two years and a half and three years they use a larger number of verbs in the past tense than in Stage 2, and form a past tense rule; use a suffix "-ed" for all of the past tense forms, e.g., *pulled* and *wiped*. Furthermore, they overgeneralize this rule, and thus, regularize verbs which should be irregular. That is, they generate forms like *comed* and *goed*, despite having previously used their correct irregular forms.[†] They sometimes generate forms like *camed* and *wented*, which is also evidence that they were not aware in Stage 2 that *went* is a past tense form of *go*. They may have considered that *went* and *go* were separate verbs.

Stage 4. After the ages of three years they become aware of the distinction between regular and irregular verbs, and regain the correct use of the irregular verbs, e.g., *broke* and *went*, that they generated in Stage 2. In this stage, they know that *went* is a past tense form of *go*. They apply the past tense rule to a correct class of verbs. If they meet a new verb, they tend to apply this rule to it like adults.

We call the four-stage progression in the acquisition of the past tense forms of verbs a **went-goed-went phenomenon** or **problem**. Ervin-Tripp (1973) reports overgeneralizations in the acquisition of plural forms of nouns, which are very similar to the one in the went-goed-went phenomenon. Such phenomena can be found also in Russian (Slobin 1966), whose cases are not indicated by word orders but by inflections. In Chapter 6, we will show that

---

[†] Braine (1971) reports that the first children of middle-class families make such overregularizations. These children are considered to have never heard overregularized forms.

BUD's category-formation/integration/disruption mechanism not only explains these phenomena but also predicts hidden parts in the four-stage progression in the went-goed-went phenomenon.

(II) Syntactic Overgeneralizations

Let us consider an overgeneralization with regard to the application of a dative movement rule, one of the transformation rules introduced by Chomsky (1965). The dative movement rule is optional and transforms sentences of type (4) into those of type (5).

(4) $NP_1 \ V \ NP_2$ to NP_3.

(5) $NP_1 \ V \ NP_3 \ NP_2$.

By this rule, the sentences in (6) are transformed to the ones in (7), respectively.

(6) a. I told a story to Bill.

b. I said a funny thing to Bill.

c. I reported the crime to the police.

d. I showed the book to Bill.

e. I demonstrated the typewriter to Bill.

(7) a. I told Bill a story.

b. *I said Bill a funny thing.

c. *I reported the police the crime.

d. I showed Bill the book.

e. *I demonstrated Bill the typewriter.

The sentences marked "*" are ungrammatical. If children overgeneralize the dative rule, and if they apply it to (6b), (6c), and (6e), then ungrammatical (7b), (7c), and (7e) should be generated. However, if children do not have access to negative examples, they never acquire adult grammars.

Hence, Baker (1979) claims that they do not form a rule like the dative rule, and that they never generate sentences like (7b), (7c), and (7e). We will discuss negative evidence, and its relationship to overgeneralizations in the next section.

Atkinson (1986) denies Baker's claim, and certifies that a child generates the following ungrammatical sentence:

(8) *I said mummy night-night.

If ungrammatical sentences with dative structures are generated by children, this means, at least, that they have formed a rule which constructs a dative structure, although they may not have the dative transformation rule that transforms (4) into (5).

(III) Semantic Overgeneralizations

Consider the following types of sentences:

(9) NP V to infinite-VP.

(10) NP_1 V NP_2 to infinite-VP.

The examples of (9) are

(11) a. *John* wanted to leave.

b. *John* asked to leave.

c. *John* begged to leave.

d. *John* promised to leave.

The examples of (10) are

(12) a. John wanted *Bill* to leave.

b. John asked *Bill* to leave.

c. John begged *Bill* to leave.

d. *John* promised Bill to leave.

e. John told *Bill* to leave.

In (11) and (12), the semantic subjects[†] of the complement sentences, i.e., to infinite-VP, are indicated by italics. In (9), the semantic subject of the complement sentence is NP. In (10), it is NP_2 for the majority of verbs[††] like *tell*, but NP_1 for verbs[†††] like *promise*. Generally, a semantic or implicit subject of a complement sentence is the NP most closely preceding it (Rosenbaum 1965). Rosenbaum calls this principle the *Minimal Distance Principle* (the MDP). In fact, all of the examples except (12d) in (11) and (12) conform to the MDP.

C. Chomsky (1969) gave a comprehension test to forty children of several ages from 5.0 to 10.0. In the situation where two dolls, Bozo and Donald, are put in front of a child, she presented him with the following set of sentences containing *promise* and *tell* without semantic cues, and asked him to indicate which doll is performing for each case.

(13) a. Bozo tells Donald to hop up and down.

Make him hop.

b. Bozo promises Donald to do a somersault.

Make him do it.

c. Donald promises Bozo to hop up and down.

Make him hop.

d. Bozo tells Donald to lie down.

Make him do it.

[†]   Semantic subjects of complement sentences are called "understood subjects" by Pollard and Sag (1987).

[††] In this case, it is said that the object, i.e., NP_2, controls the complement sentence, and the object is called a controller.

[†††] In this case, it is said that the subject, i.e., NP_1, controls the complement sentence. Hence, the subject is a controller.

      e. Bozo promises Donald to stand on the book.

      Make him do it.

      f. Donald promises Bozo to lie down.

      Have him lie down.

      g. Bozo tells Donald to do a somersault.

      Make him do it.

      h. Donald promises Bozo to stand on the book.

      Make him do it.

The additional tests indicate that all of the children have known the meanings of the words, *promise* and *tell*.

Then, she concluded that the correct assignment of the semantic subject of the complement sentence for which *promise* or *tell* subcategorizes is acquired through the following four stages:

Stage 1.   10 children

    tell - all correct

    promise - all wrong

    They assign NP_2 as subject throughout following both words.

Stage 2.   4 children

    tell - mixed

    promise - mixed

    They assign both NP_1 and NP_2 as subject following both words.

Stage 3.   5 children

    tell - all correct

    promise - mixed

    They assign NP_2 as subject consistently following *tell*, and both NP_1 and NP_2 following *promise*.

Stage 4.   21 children

    tell - all correct

promise - all correct

They assign NP$_2$ as subject following *tell*, and NP$_1$ following *promise*. In the above stages, NP$_1$ and NP$_2$ are the ones indicated in (10).

In Stage 1, an overgeneralization has occurred; that is, children have already formed a principle like the MDP, and they apply it to the sentences containing *promise* to which this principle should not be applied.

Let us compare the above four-stage progression with the went-goed-went phenomenon in (I). We express the stages in the went-goed-went phenomenon in roman, and those in the acquisition of the correct use of *tell* and *promise* in italics. *Stage 1* and *Stage 4* correspond to Stage 3 and Stage 4, respectively, but *Stage 2* and *Stage 3* are missing in the went-goed-went phenomenon. Then, how should we construe the mixed answers following *tell* and *promise* in *Stage 2*, and those following *promise in Stage 3*? Although we will construe the mixed answers by BUD's category-formation/integration/disruption mechanism in detail in Chapter 6, we give a brief construction here. Before *Stage 2* children get some negative examples, that is, sentences which contain *promise*, and to which a principle like the MDP cannot be applied. As a result, they are in confusion in *Stage 2*. These examples have exerted a bad influence upon the application of the principle to sentences containing *tell* or *promise*. The mixed answers in *Stage 2* and *Stage 3* show that they hesitate to apply the principle to sentences containing *tell* or *promise*, and that they wait for further examples. If this construction is correct, there should be hidden parts between Stage 3 and Stage 4, in which the past tense forms of regular verbs are expressed by their correct forms or base forms, and in which those of irregular verbs are expressed by their incorrect regular forms, base forms, or correct irregular forms.

(IV) Summary of Overgeneralizations

Generally, rules or principles come to be applied to correct domains in similar ways. In summary, we present a scenario from the formation of a rule to its correct use through its overgeneralization. In this scenario, the rule is restricted to one relating to **words**. That is, a child forms a rule only when he finds that some words have a common property. A set of words which he applies a rule to, or which he considers to have a common property is called a **category**.

Stage 1. A child finds properties of words separately.

Stage 2. He finds that some words have a common property, and thus, he forms a rule and a category, which is a set of these words. Let CategA be this category and P_A be the property which the words of CategA have in common. Once he forms the rule, he applies it to words which do not belong to CategA. Although it is not confirmed that these words also have P_A, he assumes that they do. Let SetB be this set of words. Let CategA′ be the following:

$$(14)\, \text{CategA}' = \text{CategA} + \text{SetB}$$

where "+" is an operator which gets a union of sets when they are disjoint. Thus, an overgeneralization has occurred, and he assumes that all the words in CategA′ have P_A. Once he forms CategA′, he forgets whether a word belonged to CategA or SetB.

Stage 3. When he gets a negative example, that is, a word in CategA′ which does not have P_A, he becomes confused, and CategA′ becomes disrupted. Thus, the words of CategA′ have lost P_A, but the rule remains and they have learned that the rule should not be overgeneralized. Then, he waits for further examples. Note that we have assumed that negative examples can be obtained by children although many researchers believe that this occurs rarely, that is, they are rarely informed by their mothers when they make syntactic errors (see Section 2.3).

Stage 4. He forms CategA″ which is guaranteed to have P_A. Then,

$$(15) \text{CategA}'' \neq \text{CategA}'$$

He never overgeneralizes the rule.

The above scenario raises the following three questions:

(i)   What are the underlying sets of CategA, CategA′, CategA″, and SetB, respectively? Do all of the words he knows constitute these underlying sets?

(ii) Does an overgeneralization of each rule take place separately? Are there any interactions among overgeneralizations of rules?

(iii) Does an overgeneralization of each rule occur only once?

In Chapter 6, we will answer these questions using BUD's category-formation/integration/disruption mechanism, and will elaborate the above scenario.

In the scenario and BUD, rules are restricted to those relating to words. In spite of this restriction, we believe that almost all of the phenomena of overgeneralizations can be explained. This is guaranteed by recent linguistic theories, such as the GB theory (Chomsky 1981, 1982, 1986a) and HPSG (Pollard 1984, 1985; Pollard and Sag 1987). These theories have a tendency to reduce the number of rewrite rules by generalizing the traditional ones which are proposed by Chomsky (1957). Instead, information about each word in the lexicon tends to be augmented. Thus, rules or principles in the above three examples of overgeneralizations can be considered, in a sense, to be related to words. For example, in HPSG, the distinction between subject and object control is accounted for on the basis of lexical entries such as those in (16) and (17).

(16) <promise, V[SUBCAT<V[SUBCAT<NP_1>], NP_2, NP_1>]>

(subject control)

(17) <tell, V[SUBCAT<V[SUBCAT<NP_2>], NP_2, NP_1>]>

(object control)

In (16) and (17), NP_1 and NP_2 are the ones indicated in (10). NP_1, indicated by italics in (16), shows that *promise* is a verb of subject control; NP_2, indicated by italics in (17), shows that *tell* is a verb of object control.

2.3. Negative Evidence

In Winston's (1975) program for learning structural descriptions of building blocks by examples, near misses, that is, negative examples, play important roles. For example, assume that the system knows that an object A, called an arch, has two properties: A is a brick, and A is supported by B and C. That is, it does not know which property is essential for A to be called an arch. Then, by receiving an example which does not have the latter property, together with negative information, the system learns that A must be supported by B and C to be called an arch.

Do children get negative examples in first language acquisition? Although mothers' or others' utterances contain several syntactic errors (Chomsky 1980), they utter neither grammatical sentences with information that the sentences are correct, nor ungrammatical sentences with information that the sentences are incorrect. Hence, children should be unable to judge which sentences are correct and which sentences are incorrect. On the other hand, how do mothers respond to their children's utterances containing some errors? Brown, Cazden, and Bellugi (1967) researched situations in which mothers gave their consent or dissent to such utterances of their children. When a mother considers that an utterance is adequate for the situation, she tends to consent to it, even if it contains some syntactic errors. For example, Eve's utterance (18) was given her mother's consent, because her mother was, in fact, curling her hair.

(18) *Her curl my hair.

On the other hand, when a mother considers that an utterance is inadequate for the situation, she tends to dissent to it, even if it is syntactically correct. For example, Salla's utterance (19) was given her mother's dissent, because the building which she called "the animal house" was a lighthouse.

(19) There's the animal house.

In this way, mothers seem to give their consent or dissent to their children's utterances on the basis of the situational adequacy of the utterances, and not on the basis of the syntactic correctness of the utterances. Therefore, many researchers believe or assume that children rarely get negative examples in first language acquisition, that is, they are rarely informed by their mothers when they make syntactic errors (for example, see Wexler and Culicover 1980; Pinker 1982, 1984; Berwick 1985).

Recently, the appropriateness of this assumption has been reexamined by Atkinson (1986), Hirsh-Pasek, Golinkoff, Braidi, and McNalty (1986), and so on. Hirsh-Pasek et al. claim that, according to Brown's data, mothers often supplement their children's utterances in which direct objects or indirect objects are missing, with the missing objects, or demand that their children make such incomplete utterances complete ones. However, mothers do not always react like this to their children's incorrect utterances. Hence, Wexler (1986) claims that mothers' reactions in not always correcting their children's incomplete utterances should confuse their children. In other words, incorrect utterances cannot be negative examples if they are not always corrected. Thus, there is no consensus among researchers concerning the question of whether or not children get negative examples in first language acquisition. Our model, named BUD, is given negative examples

24

(see Section 5.1).

2.4. Baby Talk

Utterances addressed to children by their mothers or other adults are quite different in various ways from those addressed to adults by adults. Mothers or other adults have a special way of talking to children, called **baby talk**. Because children initially cannot understand grammatically complex sentences, baby talk is necessary for communication between children and their mothers. Baby talk has the following five characteristics (Snow 1977): First, utterances in baby talk are much simpler than those addressed to adults by adults, and most of them are grammatically correct. For example, utterances addressed by adults to a group of children aged between 12 and 27 had an MLU[†] (Mean Length of Utterances in morphemes) of 4.24, while utterances addressed by adults to adults had an MLU of 11.94 (Newport 1977). Second, utterances in baby talk have very lengthy forms. Third, the previous word, phrase, or sentence is often repeated or paraphrased into an expression which is easier to understand. Fourth, mothers tend to use restricted sentence patterns. Finally, mothers adjust their utterances to the children's standard of language, and use expressions which children can understand, or expressions which are slightly more complicate than those which they can understand.

Furrow, Nelson, and Benedict (1979) and Furrow and Nelson (1986) have disputed with Newport, Gleitman, and Gleitman (1977) and Gleitman, Newport, and Gleitman (1984) about the question of whether or not there is a close correlation between maternal speech style and the characteristics of child language development. Furrow et al. point out that there are close

---

[†] An MLU, which is a unit of measuring the length of a sentence, is originally defined by Brown (1973). Murata (1984) discusses how to define an MLU for Japanese.

correlations between frequency of particular types of sentences in maternal speech and children's acquisition level of the sentence patterns, and rate highly the roles played by inputs in language acquisition. On the other hand, Newport et al. rate these roles low, and make much of the innate linguistic knowledge children have. Newport, Gleitman, and Gleitman (1977) consider as follows: If mothers followed the most desirable program for teaching children the syntax of a language, they would teach simple declarative sentences first, and then they would teach more difficult sentences, i.e., interrogative sentences or imperative sentences. However, they observed fifteen mothers, and found that 30% of the sentences they produced were declarative and 62% were interrogative or imperative. On the basis of this result, they claim that a motherese, that is, a language addressed to children by mothers, is not an adequate language for teaching the syntax of a language.

BUD has no built-in knowledge of language structures, but has a built-in procedure by which it computes the structure of a given language (see Section 1.2). Hence, it makes much of the roles played by inputs in language acquisition.

CHAPTER 3

LEARNABILITY THEORY

Gold (1967) discusses learnability or identifiability of classes of formal languages in two modes, i.e., *text presentation* and *informant presentation*. In text presentation, a learner is given a sequence of grammatical strings from the language he is learning. This is equivalent to the assumption that a child is not given negative information in primary data. In informant presentation, a learner is given a sequence of pairs comprising a string and information about whether it is grammatical or ungrammatical. This is equivalent to the assumption that a child is given negative information in primary data. He defines learnability called *identifiability in the limit* as follows:

Let A be a finite set of alphabets, and $\sum A$ represent the set of all finite strings of elements from A. A Language L signifies any subset of $\sum A$. Time is quantized and starts at a finite time.

$$(20)\, t = 1, 2, \cdots$$

At each time t, the learner is given a unit of information i_t concerning language L, and makes a guess g_t of a *name* of L based on the information it has received through time t. Thus, the learner can be considered as a function G.

$$(21)\, g_t = G\,(i_1, \cdots, i_t)$$

Two naming relations, a *tester* and a *generator*, are considered. In both cases, a name of a language, i.e., a grammar, is a Turing machine. A tester for L is a Turing machine which is a decision procedure for L. That is, it defines a function from strings to 1 or 0; it returns 1 if an input string is in L, and 0 if an input string is not in L. A tester exists if and only if L is recursive. A generator for L is a Turing machine which generates L. That is, it defines a function from positive integers to strings such that the range of this function is exactly L. A generator exists if and only if L is recursively enumerable. It is possible to effectively translate from testers to generators, but it is not possible to effectively translate from generators to testers, even for recursive languages for which both are defined. Then, L is said to be *identified in the limit* if, after some finite time, the guesses are all the same and are a name of L. A class of languages is called *identifiable in the limit* if any language of the class is identified in the limit by any allowable training sequence for this language.

He proves that with text presentation[†] only the class of finite cardinality languages is identifiable in the limit, and that with informant presentation[††] the classes are identifiable in the limit up to the class of primitive recursive

---

[†] Only an arbitrary text, one of the three types of texts Gold considers, is referred to here.

[††] Only an arbitrary informant, one of the three types of informants Gold considers, is referred to here.

languages. Both of the two claims are true with either the tester- or the generator- naming relation. Figure 3.1 shows the classes of formal languages including all of the classes from Chomsky's hierarchy (Chomsky 1963), and their relationship with Gold's learnability theory. A super-finite class of languages denotes any class which contains all languages of finite cardinality and at least one of infinite cardinality.

Let us consider what Gold's theory implies about a human's first language acquisition. Although there are no established theories about the class of natural languages, assume here that it is context-sensitive.[†] Then, natural languages cannot be acquired with text presentation but with informant presentation. Although mothers' or others' utterances contain syntactic errors, they say neither grammatical sentences with positive information, nor ungrammatical sentences with negative information. Hence, children should be unable to judge which sentences are correct and which sentences are incorrect. On the other hand, there has been no consensus among researchers concerning the question of whether or not children are informed by their mothers when they make syntactic errors (see Section 2.3).

Three approaches have been taken by researchers so that a model can learn a natural language. The first approach is to assume that children get negative examples (for example, see Anderson 1981; Selfridge 1986). The second approach is to assume that children have abundant innate knowledge about language structures, instead of assuming that they cannot get any negative examples (for example, see Berwick 1985). The third approach is to assume that children can get not only sentences but also additional information such as information about situations in which they are uttered (for

---

[†] Shieber (1985) proves that there is a construction of a sentence in the Swiss dialect of German (Swiss-German), which cannot be described by any context-free grammars.

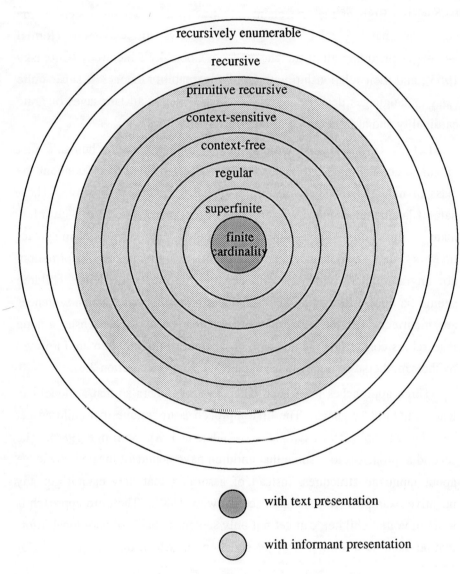

recursively enumerable

recursive

primitive recursive

context-sensitive

context-free

regular

superfinite

finite
cardinality

with text presentation

with informant presentation

Figure 3.1. Classes of Formal Languages and Their
Relationship with Gold's Learnability Theory

example, see Anderson 1977; Berwick 1985). Researchers seldom adopt only one of these approaches, but usually adopt a mixed approach. For example, Berwick (1985) adopted the second and the third approaches, and Selfridge (1986) adopted the first and the third approaches. BUD has adopted the first and the third approaches.

CHAPTER 4

BUD AND OTHER COMPUTATIONAL MODELS

4.1. Our Position on Developing BUD

Now we explain our position on developing BUD. First, we attach importance to our demand that BUD should be implemented on computers. The approach which utilizes computers makes it possible to compare the behavior of the model on a computer with the behavior of children. For example, the growth of syntax and errors at each stage can be compared. Hence, we discard or amend what cannot be implemented on computers.

Second, in its initial state, BUD has no built-in knowledge of language structures, but has a built-in procedure by which it computes the structure of a given language (see Section 1.2). In general, models based on the nativists' view can acquire the structure of a given language more easily than models based on the empiricists' view. For instance, LPARSIFAL (Berwick 1985) based on the nativists' view acquires almost complete knowledge about the structure of a given language from a relatively small number of sentences. We are not convinced of the logic which makes the nativists believe their view. Thus, by building BUD we wish to demonstrate that the empiricists' view can also explain language acquisition.

Third, BUD does not depend on any particular linguistic theory. Several models are based on particular linguistic theories. For example, Berwick's LPARSIFAL is based on the GB theory (Chomsky 1981) and Pinker's model (Pinker 1982, 1984, 1987) is based on LFG (Kaplan and Bresnan 1982). To depend on a particular linguistic theory implies to have some built-in knowledge of language structures. We want to explain language development from the standpoint of children, and not of adults (see Section 1.3).

Finally, BUD should be universal, like a baby, and should be applicable to the acquisition of any language. As an example, we discuss the acquisition of English by BUD.

4.2. Comparison between BUD and Other Models

Computer scientists, especially researchers of artificial intelligence, have recently proposed several models. These models do not satisfy us in the following points. LAS (Anderson 1977) and SNPR (Wolff 1982) are the only machine learning programs of natural languages which ignore children's behavior and the characteristics of baby talk (see Section 2.4). Berwick's LPARSIFAL has built-in knowledge of language structures. Although AMBER (Langley 1980, 1982; Langley and Carbonell 1987), ALAS (Anderson 1981), and CHILD (Selfridge 1981, 1986) try to explain children's behavior and have no built-in knowledge of language structures, they seem to be only applicable to the acquisition of languages like English and French, whose word order is fairy fixed. They cannot be the models of the acquisition of the other types of languages like Japanese and Russian, whose word order is fairly free and whose case is indicated by a word suffix. BUD aims to explain the acquisition of both types of languages. This section explains BUD's characteristics by comparing it with SNPR and CHILD.

SNPR

SNPR is given sentences as a sequence of letters, and returns a phrase structure grammar by which the observed sequence is generated. For example, when (22) is given, SNPR returns (23).

(22) JOHNLOVESMARYDAVIDHATED-
     MARYYOURUNSLOWLY ...

(23) # → (1) (2) (3) I (4) (5) (6)

1 → DAVID I JOHN

2 → LOVES I HATED

3 → MARY I SUSAN

4 → WE I YOU

5 → WALK I RUN

6 → FAST I SLOWLY

In (23), parentheses are used to distinguish non-terminal from terminal symbols. SNPR has three peculiar characteristics. First, the input sentences do not have any overt markers of segmental structure. That is, neither pauses nor punctuation marks are put between words or between sentences, and no stress is attached to input sentences. Second, texts do not contain any representations of meanings. Third, it is not provided with the intervention of any kinds of teachers. That is, it is not given negative examples and does not need anyone to provide positive or negative reinforcement of any kind. Thus, it acquires grammatical knowledge in a very data-driven manner. When applying Gold's learnability theory (see Section 3.1) to SNPR's second and third characteristics or assumptions, we find that SNPR cannot learn grammatical knowledge of natural languages.

The first characteristic or assumption contrasts with Morgan's (1986) Bracketed Input Hypothesis. This hypothesis assumes that children can readily identify hierarchical structures of sentences or construct their bracketed representations of sentences. For example, the bracketed representation as in (24) is readily constructed by children.

(24) [The little boy] [threw [a rock] [at [the dragon]]].

Morgan lists four possible sources for segmenting a sentence into phrases, i.e., isolated phrases, expansion of children's incomplete sentences by mothers, the alternation of open (content) and closed (function) class words, and prosody. Then, he proves the learnability of transformational grammars from bracketed input that are never more complex than Degree 1, that is, sentences with a single level of embedding at most. A sentence given to BUD is segmented into words beforehand, but is not segmented into phrases. BUD infers the hierarchical structures of such sentences with the help of the semantic representations given with them.

CHILD

CHILD is designed to explain the following six phenomena found in the acquisition of English as a first language.

- Comprehension precedes generation.
- Vocabulary growth rate first increases, and then decreases.
- Utterance length increases.
- Irregular words are overregularized. This phenomenon includes the went-goed-went phenomenon (see Section 2.2 (I)).
- Semantically unlikely utterances are misunderstood.

• Reversible passives are misunderstood.

CHILD does not deal with the above phenomena separately, but explains their composite progression. It has three modes: First, if only a sentence is given, CHILD considers it imperative. Second, if a sentence and its meaning represented by Schank's (1972, 1973) conceptual dependency (CD) are given, CHILD considers the sentence declarative. Third, if only a semantic representation is given, CHILD generates its description. We call the first, the second, and the third modes, an order mode, a learning mode, and a production mode, respectively. In the production mode, CHILD learns nothing, and its ability to generate a description of a given semantic representation is tested. In the order and the learning modes, CHILD learns word meanings and syntax for words which express some relations.

In the order mode, if no word[†] in a given sentence is emphasized, CHILD does not learn meanings of any words; if one word in a given sentence is emphasized, CHILD learns the meaning of the word in a highly interactive manner. That is, CHILD is provided with much intervention of a teacher. The teacher is considered to give negative examples in interaction with CHILD. When CHILD receives an imperative sentence in which one word is emphasized, it returns semantic representations which it considers to be a meaning of the sentence one by one until it gets a correct semantic representation. If CHILD returns a wrong one, the teacher says ''no'' and demands a new answer. For example, assume that CHILD receives an imperative sentence (25), returns (26) as its initial parsing of (25), and returns (27) as its final understanding of (25).

[†]   CHILD considers the endings of inflecting words as also independent words. For example, *clapped* is represented by two words, i.e., *clap* and *ed*. However, irregular words such as *gave* are treated as single words.

(25) PARENT SAYS: give papa the BALL

(26) CHILD PARSES:

    (PTRANS ACTOR (CHILD)

        OBJECT (BALL1)

        TO (TOP VAL (TABLE1))

        TIME (PRES))

(27) CHILD UNDERSTANDS:

    (ATRANS ACTOR (CHILD)

        OBJECT (BALL1)

        TO (POSS VAL (FATHER1))

        TIME (PRES))

In (25), an emphasized word, i.e., *BALL*, is indicated by capital letters. In (26), *PTRANS* signifies an action which changes the location of an object. In (27), *ATRANS* signifies an action which changes some abstract property of an object, such as a property of possession. On the assumption that a word has only a single meaning, CHILD infers a meaning of the emphasized word, i.e., *BALL*, as a common part between (26) and (27). Thus, CHILD gains (28).

(28) NEW MEANING FOR *ball*:

    ((CHILD) (BALL1) (PRES))[†]

Syntax for words which express some relations is also learned in the order mode. For example, syntax for *fed* is learned as follows. Assume that CHILD receives an imperative[††] sentence (29), returns (30) as its initial

---

[†] It is written in the original paper by Selfridge (1986) that CHILD infers a new meaning of *ball* as ((BALL1) (PRES)). However, (26) and (27) also have (CHILD) in common. Hence, we add (CHILD) to the new meaning of *ball* which is originally written in the paper.

[††] Although sentence (29) has a declarative mood, it is considered as imperative by

parsing of (29), and returns (31) as its final understanding of (29).

(29) PARENT SAYS: papa fed mama cereal

(30) CHILD PARSES:

(EAT FEEDER (MOTHER1)

FEEDEE (FATHER1)

FOOD (CEREAL1)

TIME (PAST))

(31) CHILD UNDERSTANDS:

(EAT FEEDER (FATHER1)

FEEDEE (MOTHER1)

FOOD (CEREAL1)

TIME (PAST))

Because CHILD has preliminary knowledge that *MOTHER* 1 tends to fill the *FEEDER* slot of *EAT*, and that *CHILD* tends to fill the *FEEDEE* slot of *EAT*, CHILD infers the value of *FEEDER* slot as *MOTHER* 1 in the initial parsing (30) of (29). Such preliminary knowledge is represented as semantic preferences in CHILD. Because CHILD fails to predict where the values of the *FEEDER* and the *FEEDEE* slots of *EAT* will be in sentence (29), CHILD invokes learning mechanisms, and gains the following syntax for *fed*.

(32) CHILD LEARNS SYNTAX OF *fed*:

(FEEDER) precedes *fed*, precedes (FEEDEE), precedes (FOOD),

(FEEDEE) follows (FEEDER), follows *fed*, precedes (FOOD),

CHILD. When CHILD is given only a sentence, CHILD considers it as imperative.

(FOOD) follows (FEEDER), follows *fed*, follows (FEEDEE)

In (32), (FEEDER), (FEEDEE), and (FOOD) signify the values of the *FEEDER*, the *FEEDEE*, the *FOOD* slots, respectively. The syntax CHILD learns and gains is represented as conjunctive sets of two predicates, i.e., *precedes* and *follows*, as shown in (32), and is not represented with a phrase structure grammar.

In the learning mode as well as in the order mode, CHILD learns meanings of words and syntax for words which express some relations. The difference between them is explained as follows: In the order mode, CHILD infers an intended meaning of a given sentence. In the learning mode, however, CHILD is given the meaning of a sentence with the sentence as an input.

We are dissatisfied at CHILD in the following five points, which are overcome by BUD. First, as described previously in this section, CHILD seems to be only applicable to the acquisition of languages whose word order is fairly fixed. Second, the syntax it learns is very childish, and seems to be inadequate for adult-level language, as Selfridge himself states. Third, although CHILD appears to explain the went-goed-went phenomenon, it does not handle its interaction with overgeneralizations of other rules. Overgeneralizations such as the went-goed-went phenomenon are not special, rarely-found phenomena in first language acquisition. BUD regards first language acquisition as learning the correct application of a number of rules through overgeneralizations. Hence, it treats the went-goed-went phenomenon as only one of these overgeneralizations. Furthermore, it handles this interaction with other overgeneralizations. Fourth, CHILD is provided too much intervention of a teacher in the order mode. Finally, CHILD sometimes learns syntax or meanings of words by receiving a syntactically incorrect sentence such as (33).

(33) mama go ing to the kitchen.

In (33), the copula *is* is missing just before *go* . BUD is never given syntactically incorrect sentences as grammatical ones in the three modes defined in BUD. These modes will be explained in Section 5.1. Furthermore, BUD considers all the sentences it receives as being grammatical.

4.3. BUD's Initial State

Concept formation precedes to the acquisition of syntax (Slobin 1973; Johnston 1985). In BUD's initial state, basic concepts have almost been formed and intonation patterns have already been learned.[†] Hence, BUD, as its initial state, knows basic words which stand for visible concrete things, e.g., *boy* and *kitchen*, and knows basic words which represent visible physical actions, e.g., *go*, *put*, and *throw*. Note that BUD knows only basic words. Hence, it learns the relations between unknown words and their meanings in Learning Mode or Production Mode. Furthermore, BUD, as its initial state, knows neither the structure of a given language nor the syntactic categories we often use to explain adult grammars. Moreover, BUD assumes that a form is in one-to-one correspondence with a meaning (Slobin 1985). Hence, a word has only one meaning (Bloom 1973). This assumption or restriction will be removed in later stages.

4.4. Difficult Points in Modeling Language Acquisition

(I)   Passive Grammar and Active Grammar

Grammar for comprehension and grammar for generation are often called passive grammar and active grammar, respectively. Their relationship is

---

[†]   Around the age of eight months, children have learned intonation patterns (Aitchison 1983).

still unclear (Slobin 1971). For example, children in the two-word stage can understand much more complicated utterances than two-word utterances. BUD has Order Mode for comprehension (see Section 8.1) and Production Mode for production (see Section 8.2). We believe that the difference between BUD's behavior in the two modes explain the difference between passive grammar and active grammar. On the other hand, it is known that a child's comprehension vocabulary always exceeds and encompasses his generation vocabulary (Sutton-Smith 1973). This is true of BUD, because it cannot produce any words which it does not know.

(II) Abstract Words and Mental Verbs

BUD, as its initial state, knows basic words which stand for visible concrete things and basic words which represent visible physical actions. It then learns the relations between unknown words and their meanings in Learning Mode and Production Mode. However, we do not know how to represent concepts corresponding to abstract words or mental verbs. BUD is not a model for concept formation. We do not use sentences containing such words as inputs to BUD. Hence, BUD cannot learn their syntactically correct use.

Is it also difficult for children to learn the meanings of such words and their syntactically correct use? Children talk about objects in their environment even in the stage when more than four words can be produced as an utterance (Fletcher 1985).[†] Maratsos, Fox, Becker, and Chalkley (1985) obtained a result, from comprehension tests, that children are poorer in

---

[†] When Sophie, whom Fletcher observed, was two years and four months old, the MLU calculated on the basis of the record (pp. 58-68) of her utterances was 2.53, and some of her utterances were constituted by more than four words. In this record, no abstract nouns could be found, and mental verbs were only *like* and *want*.

comprehending mental verb passives like (35) than physical action passives like (34).

(34) Superman was held by Batman.

(35) Goofy was liked by Donald.

Furthermore, they claim that mental verb passives are understood very poorly by preschool children and many early grade-school children. Thus, children also have difficulty in learning the meanings of such words and their syntactically correct use.

CHAPTER 5

THE WHOLE CONSTITUTION OF BUD

5.1. Three Modes in BUD

All of the computational models listed in Section 4.2, except SNPR, are given a sequence of pairs of sentences and their semantic representations as inputs. Then, finally if a sentence is given, they return its semantic representation as an output, and if a semantic representation is given, they return a sentence which expresses it as an output. BUD is similar to these models in this point. In the following three modes, BUD is never given syntactically incorrect sentences. Furthermore, BUD considers all of the sentences it receives as being grammatical.

In Learning Mode, BUD is given as inputs a sentence, its intonation, and its semantic representation. A pair comprising a sentence and its intonation represent the sound of the sentence. In the current version of BUD, intonation indicates only whether the end of a sentence is uttered in a rising or a falling tone. BUD then tries to analyze the structure of the sentence. If BUD can analyze it with the knowledge already acquired, BUD learns nothing. Otherwise, BUD learns some of the following:

- the syntax of a language being learned
- a meaning of an unknown word
- subcategorization information of the main word, i.e., top-level structures of sentences containing the main word
- top-level structures of sentences and global information of the language being learned
- an inflection of a word with the condition on which it inflects
- function words which a content word accompanies in a phrase with the condition on which the function words are used.

BUD has own definitions for a main word of a sentence, subcategorization information, a content word, a function word, and a phrase, which will be explained later.

In Order Mode (described in detail in Section 8.1), BUD is given as inputs a pair comprising a sentence and its intonation, and returns a semantic representation of the sentence. In this mode, BUD learns nothing, and its ability to comprehend a given sentence is tested. If it cannot analyze a sentence in Order Mode with the knowledge already acquired, it returns only pairs of content words which it found in the sentence and the concepts corresponding to them.

In Production Mode (described in detail in Section 8.2), BUD is given a semantic representation as an input, and returns a pair comprising a sentence which expresses the semantic representation and the intonation of the sentence. In this mode, if a sentence which BUD returns as an output is not corrected by us, that is, a teacher, BUD learns nothing, and its ability to generate a pair comprising a sentence which expresses a given semantic representation, and the intonation of the sentence is tested. If a correct sentence is given to BUD by a teacher after BUD returns an incorrect sentence as an output, BUD detects the difference between the correct and the incorrect sentences, and invokes disruption of categories or subcategories (see Section 6.3). Thus, the incorrect sentence that BUD returns can be regarded as a negative example, and such intervention by a teacher can be regarded as negative reinforcement. Such explicit negative examples and negative reinforcement are given to BUD only in this mode. BUD may detect an implicit negative example in a syntactically correct sentence given to it as one of the three inputs in Learning Mode (see Section 7.2.9). Explicit negative examples are minimized, and are given when the teacher considers an explicit negative example necessary. When a correct sentence is given to BUD, BUD learns the syntax of the language being learned, the meanings of unknown words, inflections of words, and so on, in this mode as well as in Learning Mode. Note that BUD may learn sounds corresponding to concepts which are values of role slots in a given semantic representation by receiving a correct sentence in Production Mode.

BUD's constitution is illustrated as Figure 5.1, where the direction of each arrow indicates the direction of data flow in Learning Mode. Each component will be briefly explained in the following section. A full description of each component will be presented in Chapter 6 and Chapter 7. The data flow in Order Mode and that in Production Mode will be presented in Section 8.1 and Section 8.2, respectively.

5.2. Data Flow in Learning Mode

Now we explain data flow in Learning Mode. Figure 5.2 illustrates the representation of each component. Assume that sentence (a), its intonation (b), and (a)'s semantic representation (c) are given as inputs in the early stage of acquisition. A sentence is a group of words (sounds), and has been segmented into words beforehand. It is usually represented in an orthographic way, but some parts of it may be represented by phonetic symbols.

48

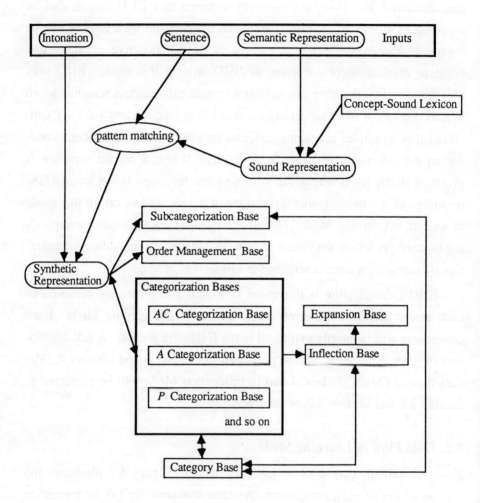

Figure 5.1. BUD's Constitution (Learning Mode)

(a) Sentence: Does the boy move the chair?
                  A   AC   P

(b) Intonation: ↑

(c) Semantic Representation:

A: boy
P: chair
AC: move
MOOD: interrogative
TIME: now

(d) Sound Representation:

A: boy
P: chair
AC: move
MOOD: interrogative
TIME: now

(e) Synthetic Representation:

ORDER: does A AC P
A: the boy(A)
P: the chair(P)
AC: move(AC)
INTONATION:
MOOD: interrogative
TIME: now

(f) Subcategorization Base:
    move - does A AC P

(g) Order Management Base:
    does A AC P - 1

(h) Inflection Base:
    $V_1 \rightarrow V_1$
    V's domain is AC.

(i) Expansion Base:
    N -> the N
    N's domain is A, G, and P.
    for A,

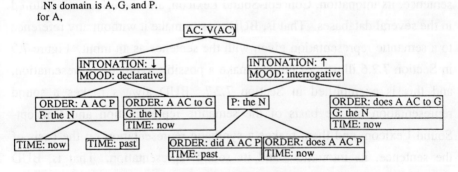

Figure 5.2. Representation of Each Component

The meaning of the sentence is represented by a semantic frame. It has pairs of role or deep case[†] slots and their values, and includes additional information about the time and the mood. The format of the semantic frame is similar to that used in Berwick's LPARSIFAL. In (c), role names A, P, and AC signify an agent, a patient, and an action, respectively. Simple concepts which are the values of the role slots, i.e., the A, the P, and the AC slots, are indicated by courier. A semantic representation given to BUD in its early stage has a flat structure, that is, the values of its role slots are only simple concepts. Hence, BUD treats a sentence as the one corresponding to one proposition. BUD cannot treat a sentence corresponding to plural propositions as such. For example, a sentence which has a noun phrase containing a relative clause, or a sentence which has a subordinate clause corresponds to plural propositions. Hence, sentences which we use as inputs in the early stage are simple ones, each corresponding to one proposition.

BUD tries to make a possible synthetic representation on the basis of a sentence, its intonation, Concept-Sound Lexicon, and the information stored in the several databases. That is, BUD tries to make it without any reference to a semantic representation given with the sentence as an input. Figure 7.9 in Section 7.2.6 illustrates how to make a possible synthetic representation, and this is exemplified in Section 7.2.7. BUD always makes a sound representation on the basis of the semantic representation and Concept-Sound Lexicon, and then, makes a synthetic representation on the basis of the sentence, its intonation, and its sound representation. That is, BUD makes the synthetic representation with reference to the semantic

---

[†] Within the general framework of case grammar, many different analyses have been proposed (for example, see Fillmore (1968), Grimes (1975)). The case system, which we have adopted in BUD, does not follow a particular analysis, but is a mixed system which several ideas of different analyses are incorporated into.

representation. If the possible synthetic representation matches the synthetic representation, that is, if BUD can analyze the sentence with the knowledge already acquired, BUD learns nothing except learning in Order Management Base. If BUD cannot make any possible synthetic representations, or if the possible synthetic representation does not match the synthetic representation, BUD learns the syntax of the language being learned, inflection of words, and so on on the basis of the synthetic representation. Now, assume that BUD cannot make any possible synthetic representations.

BUD consults Concept-Sound Lexicon, and makes a sound representation (d) from (c) by replacing the concepts which are the values of the role slots in (c) with sounds corresponding to the concepts. In Concept-Sound Lexicon, only the single forms of words which stand for visible concrete things, and the base forms of words which represent visible physical actions, are registered. The reason why the plural forms for the former words, the past tense forms for the latter words, and so on are not registered in Concept-Sound Lexicon, is based on the analysis of baby talk by Newport, Gleitman, and Gleitman (see Section 2.4). In (d), the sounds which are the values of the role slots are indicated by roman.

Next, BUD computes a synthetic representation (e) from sentence (a), its intonation (b), and its sound representation (d). By matching the values of the role slots in (d) with sentence (a), BUD determines the order of the roles, i.e., the value of the *ORDER* slot in (e); cuts out of sentence (a) a *phrase* constituted by a content word which is the value of a role slot in (d) and function words which the content word accompany in sentence (a); and stores the phrase as the value of the corresponding role slot in (e). Note that not only inputs (a), (b), and (c), but also sound representation (d) and synthetic representation (e) are temporal representations, and that BUD can give access to the inputs and the two representations only while it deals with sentence (a). Hence, when BUD deals with another sentence, they will have been lost. On the other hand, BUD can give access to the databases explained below at any time. In these databases, BUD learns syntax of the language being learned, inflections of words, and so on.

From (e), data flow into Subcategorization Base (f), Order Management Base (g), and categorization bases. In Subcategorization Base (f) (described in detail in Section 6.1 (II)), the order of the roles, i.e., the value of the *ORDER* slot in (e), is registered for the main word, i.e., *move*, of sentence (a). The definition of a main word of a sentence will also be given in Section 6.1 (II). In this base, BUD learns top-level structures of sentences containing the main word. In Order Management Base (g) (described in detail in Section 7.2.1), the order of the roles, i.e., the value of the *ORDER* slot in (e), is stored regardless of the main word, i.e., *move*, of sentence (a), and the number of sentences which have the value is also stored. In this base, BUD learns top-level structures of sentences and collects global information about the language being learned. BUD has a categorization base (in detail, see Section 6.1 (I)) for each role slot which appears in some of the synthetic representations. For example, the phrases cut out as the values of the *A* slot in the synthetic representations are stored in *A* Categorization Base. Categories are made in each categorization base on the basis of the positions of words in the phrases. We omit here examples of the representations of categorization bases (see Section 7.2).

From the categorization bases, data flow into Inflection Base (h) (described in detail in Section 6.1 (III)). When BUD finds that a word which is not registered for a concept in Concept-Sound Lexicon is used for the concept, it stored this word into Inflection Base as another word for the concept, and the condition on which it is used is also stored there. From (h), data flow into Expansion Base (i) (described in detail in Section 7.2.1), where function words which content words accompany in phrases are stored with the conditions on which the function words are used. Content words and function words will be defined in Section 7.2.1. In (h) and (i), a condition is represented as an and/or-tree (see Section 7.1), in which nodes near the root node contain more important information than those far from the root node. Data flow between Category Base and each of Subcategorization Base (f), categorization bases, and Inflection Base (h). In Category Base, categories or subcategories are formed, integrated, or disrupted (see Chapter 6). We omit here an example of the representation of Category Base (see Section 7.2).

CHAPTER 6

BUD'S CATEGORY-FORMATION/INTEGRATION/DISRUPTION MECHANISM

We explain BUD's category-formation/integration/disruption mechanism, and elaborate the scenario about an overgeneralization of a rule, which was presented in Section 2.2 (IV). As we defined there, a rule is restricted to one relating to words. That is, a child forms a rule when he finds that some words have a common property. A set of words to which he applies a rule, or which he considers to have a common property is called a category.

6.1. Formation of a Category

BUD forms a **category** simply when it finds that two or more words have a common property. A category may have subcategories. BUD forms a **subcategory** when it finds that two or more words in a category have a common property other than the property which all of the words in the category have in common. Thus, categories have *two-level* structures, and are made in the following databases.

(I)   Each Categorization Base

BUD has a categorization base for each role slot which appears in some synthetic representations. In each categorization base, phrases cut out of the sentences as the values of the corresponding role slot in synthetic representations are stored in the form of a tree, and categories are formed on the basis of the positions of words in the phrases. If a phrase is too complex, that is, if it contains more than four words, only its first four words are stored in the proper categorization base. For example, assume that the following six phrases are stored in *A* Categorization Base in this order:

(36) the boy

(37) the pretty boy

(38) the pretty girl

(39) the girl

(40) the pretty baby

(41) a pretty girl

When the values of the *A* slots in semantic representations (see (c) in Section 5.2) are simple concepts, only either the first or the last words of the *A* phrases are categorized. Which words are categorized depends on whether the value of a parameter *do-hash-begin* is *t* or *nil*.

When *do-hash-begin* is *t*, the last words are categorized as shown in Figure 6.1. In this figure and in Figure 6.2, Addr and Categ signify an address and a category, respectively. No categories are made in Step 1 and Step 2. In Step 2, *boy* is stored in two different addresses, i.e., Addr2 and Addr4, but the one in Addr2 and the one in Addr4 are guaranteed to have the same meaning because of our assumption concerning the initial state of BUD (see Section 4.3). In Step 3, BUD forms a category Categ0, whose

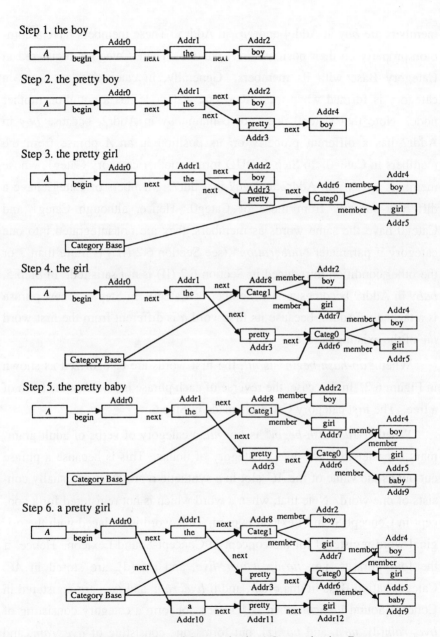

Step 1. the boy

Step 2. the pretty boy

Step 3. the pretty girl

Step 4. the girl

Step 5. the pretty baby

Step 6. a pretty girl

Figure 6.1. Formation of Categories in *A* Categorization Base
(**do-hash-begin** is *t*.)

members are *boy* in Addr4 and *girl* in Addr5. These members have a common property on their positions in *A* phrases. Then, Categ0 is registered in Category Base with its members. Generally, in categorization bases, a category is formed when more than one leaf node has a common mother node. Note that Categ0 does not contain *boy* in Addr2, because *boy* in Addr2 has a different property on its position in an *A* phrase from the members in Categ0. In Step 4, BUD forms another category Categ1, whose members are *boy* in Addr2 and *girl* in Addr7. Members of Categ1 have a different property from those of Categ0. Hence, although Categ1 and Categ0 have the same words as members, they are not integrated into one category if parameter *integration* (see Section 6.2 (II)) is more than 2 or the other condition introduced in Section 6.2 (II) is not satisfied. In Step 5, *baby* in Addr9 becomes a new member of Categ0. In Step 6, a new phrase is attached to Addr0, because its first word *a* is different from the first word *the* of the existing phrases.

When *do-hash-begin* is *nil*, the first words are categorized as shown in Figure 6.2. In this case, the reverse of each phrase is stored in the form of a tree. The first category Categ0 is made in Step 6.

Whether *do-hash-begin* is *t* or *nil*, a category of verbs of adult grammars is easier to make than a category of nouns. This is because a phrase cut out as the value of the *AC* slot in a synthetic representation usually consists of one word. Note that, when a word which is not registered for a concept in Concept-Sound Lexicon is used, THis word is replaced with the original word registered for the concept in Concept-Sound Lexicon. Hence, if the four phrases, i.e., *turn*[z], *turn, live*, and *rain*[d], are stored in *AC* Categorization Base in this order, and if *live, rain*, and *turn* are registered in Concept-Sound Lexicon, then BUD does not form a category consisting of *live, rain*[d], *turn,* and *turn*[z], but forms one consisting of *live, rain,* and *turn*. Phonetic symbols are written in brackets.

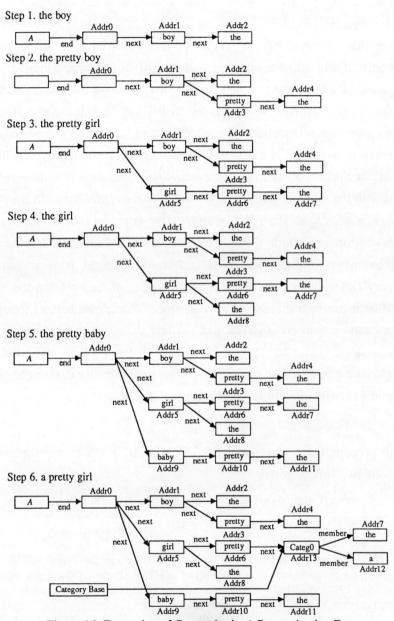

Figure 6.2. Formation of Categories in *A* Categorization Base
(**do-hash-begin** is *nil.*)

(II) Subcategorization Base

Assume that a proposition can be divided into a relation part and its argument part. Then, when a sentence corresponds to one proposition, let its main word be a head word of the phrase which expresses the relation part of the proposition, that is, a word followed by (AC) in the value of the AC slot in the synthetic representation (see (e) in Section 5.2) which corresponds to the sentence. Hence, it is a value of the AC slot in the sound representation (see (d) in Section 5.2). In Subcategorization Base, such a main word is stored with the order of roles,[†] i.e., the value of the $ORDER$ slot in the synthetic representation. The value of an $ORDER$ slot is an ordered set of role names and function words. Thus, a category called CategM which is constituted by main words of sentences is formed. CategM is registered in Category Base with its members. Every member of CategM has the property that it can be a main word of a sentence. Some members of CategM may take more than one $ORDER$ like *tell* and *show*, which are bitransitive verbs in adult grammars. When BUD finds that more than one word in CategM take an $ORDER$ in common, it forms a subcategory of CategM. For example, every member of the subcategory

$$(42)\, \text{CategM}_1 = (\text{hit, kiss, touch})$$

has the property that it can take an $ORDER = (A\ AC\ P)$. Let us consider the following two subcategories:

$$(43)\, \text{CategM}_2 = (\text{demonstrate, report, say, show, tell})$$

[†] The order of the roles stored for a main word can be considered as the subcategorization information of the word in HPSG (Pollard 1984, 1985; Pollard and Sag 1987). In HPSG, it is represented as a value of SUBCAT, which is one of the syntactic features in the lexicon.

(44) CategM$_3$ = (show, tell)

The members of CategM$_2$ and CategM$_3$ take an $ORDER$ – $(A\ AC\ O\ \text{to}\ P)$ and an $ORDER = (A\ AC\ P\ O)$, respectively. Role name O signifies an object. Although CategM$_2$ includes CategM$_3$, CategM$_2$ and CategM$_3$ are not integrated into one category if parameter *integration-for-sub* (see Section 6.2 (I)) is more than 2 or the other condition introduced in Section 6.2 (I) is not satisfied.

(III) Inflection Base

In Concept-Sound Lexicon, only the singular forms for basic words which stand for visible concrete things and the base forms for basic words which represent visible physical actions are stored initially (see Section 4.3). However, the plural forms for the former words; and the past tense forms, the present third person forms, and the past participle forms for the later words are also used in daily conversation. When BUD finds that a word which is not registered for a concept in Concept-Sound Lexicon is used for the concept, this word is stored into Inflection Base as another word for the concept, and the condition on which it is used is also stored there. From this point, if the original word registered for the concept in Concept-Sound Lexicon is used, it will be also stored into Inflection Base with the condition on which it is used. Hence, when BUD knows only one word for a concept, which is registered in Concept-Sound Lexicon for the concept, the word is not stored in Inflection Base. In most cases, phonetic forms of words used for a concept resemble each other. In English, the phonetic difference among words used for a single concept comes from suffixes of the words in most cases.

As illustrated in Figure 5.1, data flow from categorization bases into Inflection Base. Hence, when BUD finds that the same suffix can be attached to more than one member of a category made in one of categorization bases, it forms a subcategory of the category. In this case, BUD ignores the difference among the conditions on which the suffix is attached to the members of the subcategory. For example, let CategV be a category made in *AC* Categorization Base. Then, the following subcategories of CategV will be made:

(45) $CategV_1$ = (go, live, rain, turn)

(46) $CategV_2$ = (live, rain, turn)

Every member of $CategV_1$ has a property that suffix [z] can be attached to it, and every member of $CategV_2$ has a property that suffix [d] can be attached to it. Although $CategV_1$ and $CategV_2$ have three common members, they are not integrated into one subcategory of CategV if parameter *integration-for-sub* (see Section 6.2 (I)) is more than 3 or the other condition introduced in Section 6.2 (I) is not satisfied.

(IV) Categorical Properties and Subcategorical Properties

Properties of words can be divided into two types, i.e., **categorical properties** and **subcategorical properties**. Categories and subcategories are formed on the basis of categorical properties and subcategorical properties, respectively. In summary, we list below possible categorical properties and subcategorical properties.

Categorical Properties

· positions of words in phrases (see (I))

· main words of sentences (see (II))

Subcategorical Properties

· subcategorization information, i.e., *ORDERs* (see (II))

· inflections, i.e., prefixes and suffixes (see (III))

The reason why there are two kinds of properties of words is deeply related to the reason why categories have two-level structures, which we will explain in Section 6.4.

6.2. Integration of Categories

We establish here a principle called a **Uniqueness Principle**:

> For each possible categorical property, either one category or one word exists at most. For each possible subcategorical property, one **unit**, i.e., either one subcategory or one word, exists at most in a category.

The Uniqueness Principle must be always observed. Based on this assumption, we discuss two matters: integration of two subcategories of the same category and integration of two categories.

(I) Integration of Subcategories

As illustrated in Figure 6.3, assume that A and B are categories, that A_1 and A_2 are subcategories of A, that B_1, B_2, and B_3 are subcategories of B, and that two subcategories B_2 and B_3 of the same category B are integrated into a subcategory B_4 of B. Then,

$$(47) B_4 = B_2 \cup B_3$$

Let P_2, P_3, and P_4 be sets of subcategorical properties of B_2, B_3, and B_4, respectively. Then, for the Uniqueness Principle to be observed,

$$(48) P_4 = P_2 + P_3.$$

Although some members of B_4 may not be guaranteed to have all of the properties in P_4, every member is considered to have P_4. For a word to be added to B_4 as a new member, it need not be guaranteed to have all of the properties in P_4, but it must have at least one of the properties in P_4.

For two subcategories B_2 and B_3 to be integrated into B_4, both of the following conditions must be satisfied:

(i) If it has already been established by the process explained in Section 6.3 (I) that one word in B has some properties in P_4 but does not have at least one property in P_4, then they are not integrated; otherwise, they are integrated into B_4.

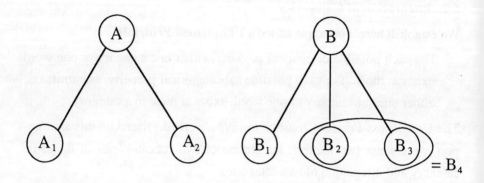

$= B_4$

Figure 6.3. Integration of Subcategories

(ii) The number of words in the intersection of B_2 and B_3 must satisfy:

$$(49) \mid B_2 \cap B_3 \mid \geq *integration-for-sub*, \quad 1 \leq *integration-for-sub* \leq *integration*,$$

where parameters $*integration-for-sub*$ and $*integration*$ are constant integers, and $*integration*$ will be introduced in (IIii).

Note that (49) is not a relative condition like (50).

$$(50) \mid B_2 \cap B_3 \mid \geq *integration-for-sub'* \mid B_2 \cup B_3 \mid, \quad 0 < *integration-for-sub'* \leq 1,$$

where $*integration-for-sub'*$ is a constant real number. If (50) were adopted as a condition, in case that both B_2 and B_3 consist of the same single word, they would be integrated. To avoid such easy integration, we have adopted (49). Note that a subcategory of a category is integrated directly with neither another category nor a subcategory of another category. However, when two categories are integrated, subcategories of one of them may be integrated with subcategories of the other.

(II) Integration of Categories

Assume that two categories A and B are integrated into a category $C = A \cup B$. Integration of categories is formulated in the similar way to integration of subcategories. Let P_A, P_B, and P_C be sets of categorical properties of A, B, and C, respectively. Then, for the Uniqueness Principle to be observed,

$$(51) P_C = P_A + P_B.$$

For A and B to be integrated into C, both of the following conditions must be satisfied:

(i) If it has already been established by the process explained in Section 6.3 (II) that more than one word has some properties in P_C but does not have at least one property in P_C, then they are not integrated; otherwise, they are integrated into C.

(ii) The number of words in the intersection of A and B must satisfy:

$$(52) \mid A \cap B \mid \geq \text{*integration*}, 1 \leq \text{*integration--for--sub*} \leq \text{*integration*},$$

where parameters *integration--for--sub* and *integration* are constant integers.

When A and B are integrated into C, some units of A will be integrated with some units of B. A unit is a subcategory whose members have some common subcategorical properties or a word which has some peculiar subcategorical properties. For the Uniqueness Principle to be observed, such integration should be performed as follows:

Step 1. Let a set of the units of A be $AU_U = (AU_1, AU_2, \cdots, AU_p)$, where p is an integer. Substitute AU_U for $AU_U{}'$. Let a set of the units of B be $BU_U = (BU_1, BU_2, \cdots, BU_q)$, where q is an integer.

Step 2. If $AU_U{}' = \varnothing$, go to Step 5; otherwise, fetch one element AU_i in $AU_U{}'$, and let a set of subcategorical properties of AU_i be P_{AU_i}.

Step 3. Collect units in BU_U, which have at least one of the properties in P_{AU_i}. Let a set of such units be $BU_S = (BU_1, BU_2, \cdots, BU_r)$, where r is an integer. Let a set of subcategorical properties of BU_j ($1 \leq j \leq r$) be P_{BU_j}.

Step 4. If $BU_S = \varnothing$, substitute $AU_U{}' - \{AU_i\}$ for $AU_U{}'$ and then, go to Step 2; otherwise, fetch one element BU_j in BU_S. For BU_j, check Case (i) and then, check Case (ii).

Case (i): It has already been established that more than one word in A has some properties in P_{AU_i} but does not have at least one property in P_{BU_j}.

If BU_j is a *subcategory* of B,

BU_j is disrupted as explained in Section 6.3 (I). Let a set of units made as a result of the disruption of BU_j be BU_{jU} = $(BU_{j1}, BU_{j2}, \cdots, BU_{js})$, where s is an integer. Let a set of subcategorical properties of BU_{jk} ($1 \le k \le s$) be $P_{BU_{jk}}$. Collect units in BU_{jU}, which have at least one of the properties in P_{AU_i}. Let a set of such units be $BU_{jS} = (BU_{j1}, BU_{j2}, \cdots, BU_{jt})$, where t is an integer. Substitute $BU_S - \{BU_j\} + BU_{jS}$ for BU_S and $BU_U - \{BU_j\} + BU_{jU}$ for BU_U. Then, go to Step 4.

If BU_j is a *word*,

create two units BU_{j1} and BU_{j2}, both of which are that word. A set of subcategorical properties of BU_{j1} is $P_{BU_{j1}} = P_{AU_i} \cap P_{BU_j}$, and that of BU_{j2} is $P_{BU_{j2}} = P_{BU_j} - P_{BU_{j1}}$. Substitute $BU_S - \{BU_j\} + \{BU_{j1}\}$ for BU_S, and $BU_U - \{BU_j\} + \{BU_{j1}, BU_{j2}\}$ for BU_U. Then, go to Step 4.

Case (ii): It has already been established that more than one word in B has some properties in P_{BU_j} but does not have at least one property in P_{AU_i}.

If AU_i is a *subcategory* of A,

AU_i is disrupted. Let a set of units made as a result of the disruption of AU_i be $AU_{iU} = (AU_{i1}, AU_{i2}, \cdots, AU_{iu})$, where u is an integer. Substitute $AU_U - \{AU_i\} + AU_{iU}$ for AU_U, and $AU_U' - \{AU_i\} + AU_{iU}$ for AU_U'. Then, go to Step 2.

If AU_i is a *word*,

create two units AU_{i1} and AU_{i2}, both of which are that word. A set of subcategorical properties of AU_{i1} is $P_{AU_{i1}} = P_{AU_i} \cap P_{BU_j}$, and that of AU_{i2} is $P_{AU_{i2}} = P_{AU_i} - P_{AU_{i1}}$. Substitute $AU_U - \{AU_i\} + \{AU_{i1}, AU_{i2}\}$ for AU_U, and $AU_U' - \{AU_i\} + \{AU_{i1},$

AU_{i2}} for $AU_U{}'$. Then, go to Step 2.

If neither (i) nor (ii) is satisfied, substitute BU_S - {BU_j} for BU_S, and then, go to Step 4.

Step 5. If $AU_U = \emptyset$, BU_U is a set of the units of C. Let a set of the units of C be $CU_U = (CU_1, CU_2, \cdots, CU_v)$, where v is an integer. Let a set of subcategorical properties of CU_i ($1 \leq i \leq v$) be P_{CU_i}. Then, CU_i satisfies a condition like (Ii), that is, BUD does not know a word in C such that it has some properties in P_{CU_i} but does not have at least one property in P_{CU_i}. If $AU_U \neq \emptyset$, fetch one element AU_i in AU_U.

Step 6. Let a set of subcategorical properties of AU_i be P_{AU_i}. Collect units in BU_U, which have at least one of the properties in P_{AU_i}. Let a set of such units be $BU_S = (BU_1, BU_2, \cdots, BU_w)$, where w is an integer. Let a set of subcategorical properties of BU_j ($1 \leq j \leq w$) be P_{BU_j}. For each of AU_i and BU_j ($1 \leq j \leq w$), if this unit is a word, transform it to a set consisting only of that word. Then, $CU_i{}' = AU_i{}' \cup BU_1{}' \cup BU_2{}' \cup \cdots \cup BU_w{}'$. For $CU_i{}'$ to be made like this, there are no conditions concerning the number of words in the intersection among AU_i and BU_j ($1 \leq j \leq w$), which, in other words, need not satisfy a condition like (49) of (Iii). If $CU_i{}'$ is a set consisting of one word, transform it to a unit as a word. Thus, CU_i is obtained. Let a set of subcategorical properties of CU_i be P_{CU_i}. Then, $P_{CU_i} = P_{AU_i} \cup P_{BU_1} \cup P_{BU_2} \cup \cdots \cup P_{BU_w}$. Substitute AU_U - {AU_i} for AU_U, and BU_U - BU_S + {CU_i} for BU_U. Then, go to Step 5.

Note that category C inherits information about negative examples from A and B.

6.3. Disruption of a Category

(I) Disruption of a Subcategory

Let us consider the following situation illustrated in Figure 6.4, where A, B, C, D, E, F, and G are subcategories of category U:

After A and B were integrated into $C' = A \cup B$, a set of words α was added to C', and then $C = C' + \alpha$ was obtained. After D and E were integrated into $F' = D \cup E$, a set of words β was added to F', and then $F = F' + \beta$ was obtained. After C and F were integrated into $G' = C \cup F$, a set of words γ was added to G', and then $G = G' + \gamma$ has been obtained.

Assume that each of A, B, D, and E has only one subcategorical property. Let P_A, P_B, P_D, and P_E be properties of A B, D, and E, respectively. Then all of the words in G are considered to have these four properties. Now assume that BUD has found one word in G which has P_B, but does not have P_A. Then, subcategory G is disrupted. A word remembers a number of subcategories to which it recently belonged. Let parameter *disruption-for-sub*, which is a non-negative integer, indicate this number. The state to be recovered depends on *disruption-for-sub*.

(i) If *disruption-for-sub* = 0, BUD restarts from the state where BUD knows nothing about any word in G except the categorical properties of U.

(ii) If *disruption-for-sub* = 1, γ and C are canceled. BUD restarts from the state where F remains, but where BUD knows nothing about any word in γ and C except the categorical properties of U.

(iii) If *disruption-for-sub* ≥ 2, γ and α are canceled. BUD restarts from the best state where A, B, and F remain, but where BUD knows nothing about any word in γ and α except the categorical properties of U.

70

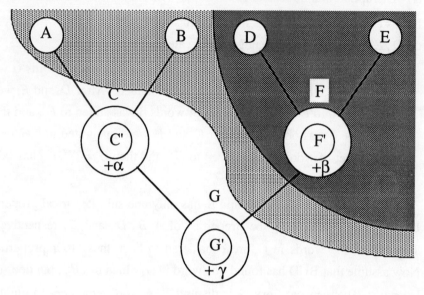

disruption-for-sub = 2   *disruption-for-sub* = 1

Figure 6.4. Disruption of a Subcategory

In the above three cases, category U will remember that a word exists in U such that it has P_B, but does not have P_A. However, U will not remember which word in U is problematic. Note that the Uniqueness Principle is observed even if G is disrupted.

(II) Disruption of a Category

Disruption of a category is performed in a similar way to disruption of a subcategory. A word remembers a number of categories to which it recently belonged. Let parameter *disruption*, which is a non-negative integer, indicate this number. The state to be recovered depends on *disruption*. Assume that two categories A and B were integrated into a category C, and that C has been disrupted. Further assume that BUD restarts from the state where A and B remain. Then, BUD knows words which constitute A and B respectively, but does not recover subcategories of A and B. That is, BUD knows nothing about any word in A except the categorical properties of A, and about any word in B except the categorical properties of B.

6.4. Discussion

At first, we explain the reason why categories do not have flat (or one-level) structures, but have two-level structures. Children seem to make more errors in the subcategorical properties of words than in the categorical properties of words. Almost all children who learn English as their native language make errors with suffixes of nouns and verbs. On the other hand, errors in the main words of sentences or in the positions of words in phrases are rarely reported. BUD, in which categories have two-level structures, can explain the different frequencies of the two types of errors.

Three models, i.e., AMBER (Langley 1980, 1982; Langley and Carbonell 1987), CHILD (Selfridge 1981, 1986) and a connectionist model by Rumelhalt and McClelland (1986, 1987), deal with the went-goed-went phenomenon as an independent one. However, BUD deals with the interactions between this and other overgeneralizations (see Section 2.2 (IVii)). Now assume that all the verbs which BUD knows constitute $CategV$, and that its subcategory $CategV_1$, whose members have a subcategorical property that suffix [d] is used for the past tense, and another subcategory $CategV_2$ of $CategV$ are integrated into $CategV_3$. All of the words in $CategV_3$ are considered to have the property that suffix [d] is used for the past tense. Then, only if $CategV_3 = CategV$ do, all of the verbs BUD knows have suffix [d] for the past tense in Stage 3 (see Section 2.2 (I)); otherwise, in Stage 3, there exists more than one verb such that suffix [d] is not used for the past tense. Next, assume that $CategV$ is integrated with another category $CategX$, and that, as a result, $CategV_1$ is integrated with a subcategory of $CategX$. Then, suffix [d] may be used for a word which is not a verb in Stage 3.

Now, we answer the questions (i) and (iii) in Section 2.2 (IV). For (i), each of the underlying sets of $CategA$, $CategA'$, $CategA''$, and $SetB$ is a set constituted by all of the words the child knows, or a category to which it belongs if it is a subcategory. The answer to (iii) is *no*, because a subcategory with a particular property may repeatedly undergo integration with another subcategory and restart as a result of the disruption.

CHAPTER 7

COMPARISON BETWEEN LANGUAGE PHENOMENA AND BUD'S BEHAVIOR

7.1. Inferences and Six Parameters

BUD has six parameters as its variable parts: *do-hash-begin*, *depth*, *integration*, *integration-for-sub*, *disruption*, and *disruption-for-sub*. These parameters influence various aspects of inferences made by BUD.

Parameter *do-hash-begin* (see Section 6.1 (I)) influences three aspects of inferences. Its value is *t* or *nil*. First, it determines how to cut out phrases from a sentence (see Section 7.2.1). Second, it determines whether the first or the last words in phrases are categorized (see Section 6.1 (I)). Third, when a category has more than one categorical property related to the same categorization base, it determines how to compare such categorical properties (see Section 7.2.6).

Parameter *depth* introduced here influences two aspects of inferences. Its value is a non-negative integer. First, it controls the amount of information which BUD keeps in Expansion Base and Inflection Base about the sentences which BUD has received up to the present. When BUD finds that a word which is not registered for a concept in Concept-Sound Lexicon is used for the concept, this word is stored into Inflection Base as another word for the concept, together with the condition on which it is used (see Section 6.1 (III)). In Expansion Base, function words which content words accompany in phrases are stored together with conditions on which they are used (see Section 7.2.1). Conditions for the application of such rules stored in Inflection Base or Expansion Base are represented as and/or-trees. We define the **node** as a group of subconditions which must be satisfied at the same time, that is, what is called an and-subtree, and the **depth** of a tree as the maximum distance from the root node to the leaf nodes. For example, the depth of a tree consisting of only a root node is 0. In Figure 7.1, the condition on which a content word included in category N accompanies function word *the* in A phrases is represented as and/or-trees of depth 0, 1, 2, and 3 in (i), (ii), (iii), and (iv), respectively. This condition is stored in Expansion Base.

If tree (i) is stored there as the condition, BUD considers that the subcondition in node (a) must be satisfied for N to accompany *the*.

If tree (ii) is stored there, BUD considers that either of the following must be satisfied for N to accompany *the*:

- the subcondition in (a) and the two subconditions in (b)
- the subcondition in (a) and the two subconditions in (c)

If tree (iii) is stored there, BUD considers that one of the following must be satisfied for N to accompany *the*:

Expansion Base:
  N -> the N
  N's domain is A, G, and P.
  for A,

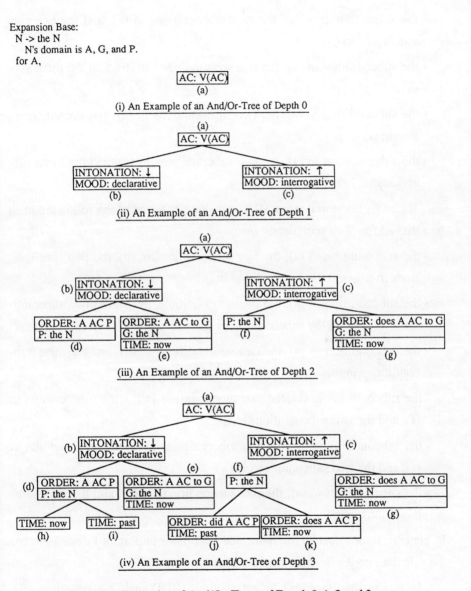

Figure 7.1. Examples of And/Or-Trees of Depth 0, 1, 2 and 3

- the subcondition in (a), the two subconditions in (b), and the two subconditions in (d)

- the subcondition in (a), the two subconditions in (b), and the three subconditions in (e)

- the subcondition in (a), the two subconditions in (c), and the subcondition in (f)

- the subcondition in (a), the two subconditions in (c), and the three subconditions in (g)

If tree (iv) is stored there, BUD considers that one of the following must be satisfied for N to accompany *the*:

- the subcondition in (a), the two subconditions in (b), the two subconditions in (d), and the subcondition in (h)

- the subcondition in (a), the two subconditions in (b), the two subconditions in (d), and the subcondition in (i)

- the subcondition in (a), the two subconditions in (b), and the three subconditions in (e)

- the subcondition in (a), the two subconditions in (c), the subcondition in (f), and the two subconditions in (j).

- the subcondition in (a), the two subconditions in (c), the subcondition in (f), and the two subconditions in (k).

- the subcondition in (a), the two subconditions in (c), and the three subconditions in (g)

In general, nodes near to the root node bear more important information for the rule than nodes far from the root node.

In Expansion Base and Inflection Base, BUD makes a condition tree whose depth is *depth* at most. The next section will explain how to make a tree. The larger *depth* is, the more information BUD keeps in the two bases about the sentences it has received up to the present. For example, when *depth* is extremely large, BUD may keep information about all of the sentences to which a rule is applied.

Second, *depth* influences the number of possible synthetic representations BUD makes on the basis of the condition on the application of a rule (see Section 7.2.6 and Section 7.2.7). A possible synthetic representation can be regarded as a hypothesis BUD makes on the basis of the knowledge already acquired. For example, assume that $mother(A) \in N$, and that BUD tries to apply rule ($N \rightarrow$ the N) in Figure 7.1 to $mother(A)$. Then, when *depth* = 0, 1, 2, and 3, BUD makes one, two, four, and six possible synthetic representations, respectively. In general, the larger *depth* is, the larger the number of possible synthetic representations BUD makes on the basis of the condition on the application of a rule is.

Parameter *integration−for−sub* (see Section 6.2 (I)) determines the minimum number of words which the intersection of two subcategories of a category must have when they are integrated into a subcategory of the category. Its value is a positive integer.

Parameter *integration* (see Section 6.2 (II)) determines the minimum number of words which the intersection of two categories must have when they are integrated into a category. Its value is a positive integer.

A word remembers a number of subcategories to which it recently belonged. Parameter *disruption−for−sub* (see Section 6.3 (I)) indicates this number, and determines the state to be recovered when a subcategory is disrupted. Its value is a non-negative integer.

A word remembers a number of categories to which it recently belonged. Parameter *disruption* (see Section 6.3 (II)) indicates this number, and determines the state to be recovered when a category is disrupted. Its value is a non-negative integer.

We want to decide the values of these six parameters by comparing BUD's behavior with children's behavior. The six parameters may be related to restriction on children's short-term memory or restriction on their ways of thought. Hence, the parameters may not be independent of each other.

7.2. BUD's Behavior in Getting the First Nine Sample Sentences

By presenting BUD's behavior in getting the first nine sample sentences, this section explains in detail how BUD learns the syntax of the language being learned, meanings of unknown words, inflections of words, and so on in Learning Mode, how it forms categories or subcategories, how an over-generalization occurs as a result of the integration of subcategories, and how a subcategory is disrupted. BUD's behavior in the early stage is exemplified below. As described in Section 5.2, sentences used as inputs in the early stage are simple ones, each corresponding to one proposition. How temporary representations are made and how the several databases in BUD are used are also shown below in detail.

Now, assume that BUD receives the following nine sentences in this order from the initial state:

(54) Does the boy kiss the girl?

(55) Does the girl go to the kitchen?

(56) The mother kiss*iz* the father.

(57) The father open*z* the door.

(58) The boy touch*iz* the girl.

(59) Does the mother touch the boy?

(60) Does the father touch the mother?

(61) The cat touch*iz* the girl.

(62) The boy move*z* the chair.

In the above sentences, phonetic symbols are indicated by italics. Furthermore, assume that the six parameters have the following values:

(63) $*do-hash-begin* = t$

(64) $*depth* = 1$

(65) $*integration-for-sub* = 2$

(66) $*integration* = 2$

(67) $*disruption-for-sub* = 1$

(68) $*disruption* = 1$

In Concept-Sound Lexicon, the following pairs of concepts and sounds are registered:

(69) boy - boy

(70) chair - chair

(71) door - door

(72) father - father

(73) girl - girl

(74) go - go

(75) kick - kick

(76) kiss - kiss

(77) kitchen - kitchen

(78) mother - mother

(79) move - move

(80) open - open

(81) touch - touch

In the above pairs, concepts and sounds are indicated by courier and roman, respectively. We assume that the concepts in Concept-Sound Lexicon have already been formed in the initial state, and that the correspondences between concepts and words (sounds) have already been learned in this state. In this state, only the single forms of words which stand for visible concrete things and the base forms which represent visible physical actions are registered in Concept-Sound Lexicon.

7.2.1. BUD's Behavior in Getting the First Sample Sentence

We reintroduce Figure 5.1 as Figure 7.2. This illustrates data flow in BUD's early stage. Assume that, as shown in Figure 7.3, BUD is given the first sentence (54), its intonation, and its semantic representation as inputs. The sentence is a group of words (sounds), and has been segmented into words beforehand. The intonation indicates that the end of the sentence is uttered in a rising tone. The semantic representation corresponds to one proposition, and a semantic frame is adopted as a semantic representation. Role names A, P, and AC signify an agent, a patient, and an action, respectively. The values of the role slots are simple concepts, which are indicated by courier.

BUD searches the sentence for words which are registered for concepts in Concept-Sound Lexicon or Inflection Base. Inflection Base, which will be explained later in this section, is empty now. Hence, BUD finds three words, *boy*, *kiss*, and *girl*, which are registered in Concept-Sound Lexicon. Next, BUD searches these three words for ones registered in Subcategorization Base as words which can be main words of sentences. Subcategorization Base, which will be explained later in this section, is empty now. Hence, BUD cannot find such words. Thus, BUD cannot analyze the first sentence (54) with the knowledge already acquired.

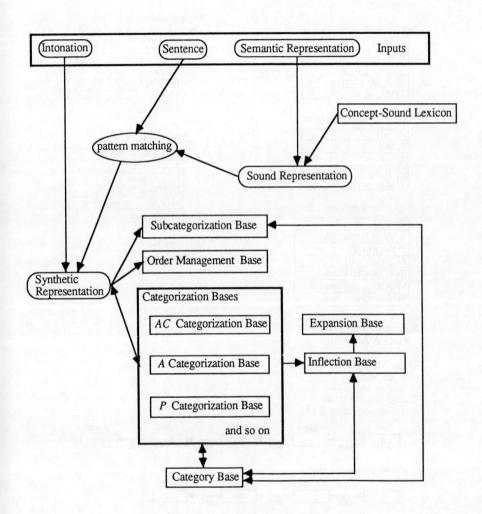

Figure 7.2. Data Flow in BUD's Early Stage

Sentence 1: Does the boy kiss the girl?
                    A AC   P

Intonation: ↑

Semantic Representation:

A: boy
P: girl
AC: kiss
MOOD: interrogative
TIME: now

Sound Representation:

A: boy
P: girl
AC: kiss
MOOD: interrogative
TIME: now

Synthetic Representation:

ORDER: A AC P
A: does the boy(A)
P: the girl(P)
AC: kiss(AC)
INTONATION: ↑
MOOD: interrogative
TIME: now

Subcategorization Base:
kiss - A AC P

Order Management Base:
A AC P - 1

Categorization Bases
A Categorization Base:

Inflection Base:
empty

Expansion Base:
boy(A) -> does the boy(A)

ORDER: A AC P
P: the girl(P)
AC: kiss(AC)
INTONATION: ↑
MOOD: interrogative
TIME: now

girl(P) -> the girl(P)

ORDER: A AC P
A: does the boy(A)
AC: kiss(AC)
INTONATION: ↑
MOOD: interrogative
TIME: now

Category Base:
empty

A Categorization Base:

```
            Addr0          Addr1          Addr2          Addr3
 ┌─────┐        ┌──────┐        ┌──────┐        ┌──────┐
 │  A  │  begin │      │  next  │ does │  next  │ the  │  next  │ boy  │
 └─────┘        └──────┘        └──────┘        └──────┘
```

P Categorization Base:

```
            Addr4          Addr5          Addr6
 ┌─────┐        ┌──────┐        ┌──────┐
 │  P  │  begin │      │  next  │ the  │  next  │ girl │
 └─────┘        └──────┘        └──────┘
```

AC Categorization Base:

```
            Addr7          Addr8
 ┌─────┐        ┌──────┐
 │ AC  │  begin │      │  next  │ kiss │
 └─────┘        └──────┘
```

Figure 7.3. BUD's Behavior in Getting the First Sample Sentence

Now, a sound representation is computed from the semantic representation and Concept-Sound Lexicon, and then, a synthetic representation is computed from the sentence, its intonation, and its sound representation. When BUD has made progress in learning English syntax, BUD will be able to make a possible synthetic representation without any reference to the sound representation, that is, without any reference to the semantic representation given with the sentence as an input. In other words, BUD will be able to make a possible synthetic representation on the basis of the sentence, its intonation, Concept-Sound Lexicon, and information stored in the several databases.

BUD consults Concept-Sound Lexicon, and makes a sound representation from the semantic representation by replacing the concepts as the values of the role slots, i.e., the A, the P, and the AC slots, in the semantic representation with sounds corresponding to the concepts. In the sound representation, the sounds which are the values of the role slots are indicated by roman. The sound representation inherits the values of the $MOOD$ and the $TIME$ slots from the semantic representation.

A synthetic representation is computed from the sentence, its intonation, and its sound representation. BUD determines the value of the $ORDER$ slot and the values of the role slots, i.e., the A, the P, and the AC slots, in the synthetic representation by matching the values of the role slots in the sound representation with the sentence. First, BUD searches the sentence for the words (sounds) of the role slots in the sound representation. Then, as illustrated in Figure 7.3, three underlined words are found in the sentence. From the left, they are arranged in order of the value of the A slot, the value of the AC slot, and the value of the P slot. Thus, the value of the $ORDER$ slot in the synthetic representation is determined as (A AC P). Because parameter *do-hash-begin* is t, the values of the A, the AC, and the P slots in the synthetic representation are determined as follows. The value of the A slot in the synthetic representation is the words from the beginning of the sentence to the word of the A slot, i.e, *boy*, in the sound representation, that is, *does the boy*(A). (A) indicates that the word which precedes it is the value of the A slot in the sound representation, and is registered for some concept in Concept-Sound Lexicon. The value of the A slot in the synthetic representation, which is cut out of the sentence like this, is called an A **phrase** of the sentence. The value of the AC slot is the words from the word next to *boy* to the word of the AC slot, i.e., *kiss*, in the sound representation, that is, a single word *kiss*(AC). Hence, the single word *kiss* constitutes an AC phrase of the sentence. The value of the P slot is the words from the word next to *kiss* to the word of the P slot, i.e., *girl*, in the sound representation, that is, *the girl*(P). These words constitute a P phrase of the sentence. If there were some words following *girl* in the sentence, these words would also be included in the P phrase, which is the last element of the value of the *ORDER* slot.

If parameter **do-hash-begin** were *nil*, the values of the A, the AC, and the P slots in the synthetic representation would be determined as follows. The value of the P slot in the synthetic representation would be the words from the word of the P slot, i.e., *girl*, in the sound representation to the end of the sentence, that is, a single word *girl*(P). The value of the AC slot in the synthetic representation would be the words from the word of the AC slot, i.e., *kiss*, in the sound representation to the word followed by *girl*, that is, *kiss*(AC) *the*. The value of the A slot in the synthetic representation would be the words from the word of the A slot in the sound representation to the word followed by *kiss*, that is, a single word *boy*(A). However, because there are some words preceding *boy* in the sentence, these words, i.e., *does the*, would also be included in the A phrase, which is the first element of the value of the *ORDER* slot. Thus, the A phrase would be constituted by *does the boy*(A).

The synthetic representation inherits the values of the *MOOD* and the *TIME* slots from the sound representation, and involves information about the intonation, which indicates that the end of the sentence is uttered in a rising tone.

From the synthetic representation, data flow into Subcategorization Base, Order Management Base, and categorization bases. In these databases, BUD learns the syntax of the language being learned, inflections of words, and so on.

In Subcategorization Base, the value of the *ORDER* slot, i.e., (*A AC P*), in the synthetic representation is registered for the main word, i.e., *kiss*, of the sentence. The main word of the sentence is the word followed by (*AC*) in the value of the *AC* slot in the synthetic representation (see Section 6.1 (II)). Hence, it is the value of the *AC* slot in the sound representation. In this base, BUD learns top-level structures of sentences containing the main word. In other words, this base collects subcategorization information of the main word. This subcategorization information is one of the subcategorical properties of words. Thus, BUD has learned, by getting the first sentence, that sentences containing *kiss* can have a top-level structure (*A AC P*).

In Order Management Base, the value of the *ORDER* slot, i.e., (*A AC P*), in the synthetic representation is stored regardless of the main word, i.e., *kiss*, of the sentence, and the number, i.e., 1, of sentences which have the value is also stored. In this base, only the ten most frequent values of the *ORDER* slots are stored. Here, BUD learns top-level structures of sentences and collects global information of the language being learned. For example, BUD may learn that a sentence usually has an *A* phrase as its first phrase, or that the language being learned is order-free. BUD uses, only in Order Mode, the information in this base, when BUD does not know which the main word of a given sentence is.

BUD has a categorization base for each role slot which appears in some synthetic representations. In dealing with the first sentence (54), BUD stores the *A* phrase, the *P* phrase, and the *AC* phrase into *A* Categorization Base, *P* Categorization Base, and *AC* Categorization Base, respectively. In each categorization base, categories will be formed on the basis of the positions of words in the phrases which BUD has received up to the present. Because *do-hash-begin* is *t*, the last words of the phrases will be categorized. However, no categories are formed in this state on the basis of such categorical properties of words.

From the categorization bases, data flow into Inflection Base. When BUD finds that a word which is not registered for a concept in Concept-Sound Lexicon is used for the concept, this word is stored into Inflection Base as another word for the concept, together with the condition on which it is used. The word, i.e., *boy*, followed by (*A*) in the *A* phrase of the first sentence (54), the word, i.e., *girl*, followed by (*P*) in the *P* phrase of (54), and the word, i.e., *kiss*, followed by (*AC*) in the *AC* phrase of (54) are registered for concepts boy, girl, and kiss, respectively, in Concept-Sound Lexicon. Hence, in this state, no words are stored into Inflection Base.

From Inflection Base, data flow into Expansion Base, where function words which content words accompany in phrases are stored with the conditions on which they are used. **Content words** are defined as words (sounds) registered for some concepts in Concept-Sound Lexicon or Inflection Base. Any words which are not content words in sentences are considered as **function words**. In the *A* phrase of (54), *boy* is a content word, and *does* and *the* are function words. In the *P* phrase of (54), *girl* is a content word, and *the* is a function word. The *AC* phrase of (54) is constituted by only a content word, i.e., *kiss*. As illustrated in Figure 7.3, the condition on which content word *boy*(*A*) accompanies function words *does the* is stored into this base in the form of an and/or-tree of depth 0. Rule (boy(A) $\rightarrow$ does the boy(A)) indicates that content word *boy(A)* can accompany function words *does the* which it follows. In Section 7.1, the depth of a tree was defined as the maximum distance from the root node to the leaf nodes. The tree consists of only a root node which has six subconditions. BUD considers that all of the six subconditions must be satisfied for *boy(A)* to accompany *does the*. Similarly, the condition on which content word *girl(P)* accompanies function word *the* is stored into this base in the form of an and/or-tree of depth 0.

Data flow between Category Base and each of Subcategorization Base, categorization bases, and Inflection Base. In Category Base, categories or subcategories are formed, integrated, or disrupted (see Chapter 6). Because no categories are made in Subcategorization Base or categorization bases, no subcategories are made in Subcategorization Base or Inflection Base. Thus, neither categories nor subcategories are stored into Category Base.

7.2.2. BUD's Behavior in Getting the Second Sample Sentence

Assume that, as shown in Figure 7.4, BUD is given the second sentence (55), its intonation, and its semantic representation as inputs. In the semantic representation, role name *G* signifies a goal. BUD searches the sentence for content words. As shown in Figure 7.3, Inflection Base is now empty. Hence, BUD finds three words, i.e., *girl*, *go*, and *kitchen*, which are registered in Concept-Sound Lexicon. Next, BUD searches these three words for ones registered in Subcategorization Base as words which can be main words of sentences. As shown in Figure 7.3, only *kiss* is registered as such in Subcategorization Base. Hence, BUD cannot find such words. Thus, BUD cannot analyze the second sentence (55) with the knowledge already acquired.

88

Sentence 2: Does the <u>girl</u> go to the <u>kitchen</u>?
                 A AC   G

Intonation: ↑

Semantic Representation:

A: girl
G: kitchen
AC: go
MOOD: interrogative
TIME: now

Sound Representation:

A: girl
G: kitchen
AC: go
MOOD: interrogative
TIME: now

Synthetic Representation:

ORDER: A AC G
A: does the girl(A)
G: to the kitchen(G)
AC: go(AC)
INTONATION: ↑
MOOD: interrogative
TIME: now

Subcategorization Base:
Categ0 = (go, kiss) ⟹ Categ3 = (go, kiss)
Categ0/go - A AC G ⟹ Categ3/go - A AC G
Categ0/kiss - A AC P ⟹ Categ3/kiss - A AC P

Order Management Base:
A AC G - 1
A AC P - 1

Inflection Base:
empty

Expansion Base:
Categ1 -> does the Categ1
Categ1's domain is A.

AC: Categ3
INTONATION: ↑
MOOD: interrogative
TIME: now

ORDER: A AC P	ORDER: A AC G
P: the girl(P)	G: to the kitchen(G)

kitchen(G) -> to the kitchen(G)

ORDER: A AC G
A: does the Categ1
AC: Categ3
INTONATION: ↑
MOOD: interrogative
TIME: now

girl(P) -> the girl(P)

ORDER: A AC P
A: does the Categ1
AC: Categ3
INTONATION: ↑
MOOD: interrogative
TIME: now

Category Base:
✓Categ0 = (go, kiss)
    Categ0's domain is Subcategorization Base.
Categ1 = (boy, girl)
    Categ1's domain is A.
✓Categ2 = (go, kiss)
    Categ2's domain is AC.
Categ0 and Categ2 are integrated into Categ3.
Categ3 = (go, kiss)
    Categ3's domain is Subcategorization Base
    and AC.

Figure 7.4. BUD's Behavior in Getting the Second Sample Sentence

Categorization Bases
A Categorization Base:

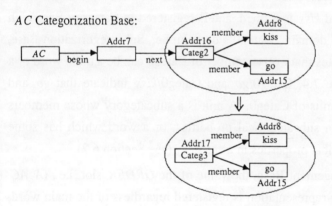

G Categorization Base:

P Categorization Base:
See Figure 7.3.

AC Categorization Base:

Figure 7.4. BUD's Behavior in Getting the Second Sample Sentence (Continued)

Next, a sound representation is computed from the semantic representation and Concept-Sound Lexicon, and then, a synthetic representation is computed from the sentence, its intonation, and its sound representation in the same way as the computation of the synthetic representation for the first sentence (54).

In Subcategorization Base, the value of the *ORDER* slot, i.e., (*A AC G*), in the synthetic representation is registered for the main word, i.e., *go*, of the second sentence (55). Because BUD has learned that each of two words, i.e., *go* and *kiss*, can be a main word of a sentence, Categ0 whose members are *go* and *kiss* is formed, and is registered in Category Base with its members and its domain. Categ0's domain, i.e., Subcategorization Base, in Figure 7.4 indicates that every member of Categ0 can be a main word of a sentence. In Figure 7.4, Categ0/*go* and Categ0/*kiss* indicate that *go* and *kiss* are words as units of Categ0. A unit is a subcategory whose members have some common subcategorical properties, or a word which has some peculiar subcategorical properties in a category (see Section 6.2).

In Order Management Base, the value of the *ORDER* slot, i.e., (*A AC G*), in the synthetic representation is registered regardless of the main word, i.e., *go*, of the sentence, and the number, i.e., 1, of sentences which have the value is also stored.

In categorization bases, two categories are formed. BUD forms in *A* Categorization Base, a category Categ1 whose members are *boy* in Addr3 and *girl* in Addr9, and in *AC* Categorization Base, a category Categ2 whose members are *kiss* in Addr8 and *go* in Addr15. These two categories are registered in Category Base with their members and their domains. Categ1's domain, i.e., *A*, in Figure 7.4 indicates that all the members of Categ1 can occupy the same position in *A* phrases, and Categ2's domain, i.e., *AC*, in Figure 7.4 indicates that all the members of Categ2 can occupy the same position in *AC* phrases.

Now, three categories are stored in Category Base. The number of words in the intersection of Categ0 and Categ2 is two, as given by

(82) | Categ0 ∩ Categ2 | = | (go, kiss) | = 2.

Because parameter *integration* = 2, and because the other condition (i) introduced in Section 6.2 (II) is also satisfied, Categ0 and Categ2 are integrated into Categ3.

(83) Categ3 = Categ0 ∪ Categ2 = (go, kiss)

Hence, Categ0 in Subcategorization Base and Categ2 in *AC* Categorization Base are replaced with Categ3, and the entries for Categ0/*go* and Categ0/*kiss* in Subcategorization Base are replaced with the entries for Categ3/*go* and Categ3/*kiss*, respectively. The entries for Categ0 and Categ2 are removed from Category Base, and Categ3 is stored there with its members and its domain. Every member in Categ3 is considered to have both a categorical property that it can be a main word of a sentence, and a categorical property that it can be a single word constituting an *AC* phrase. Thus, Categ0's domain and Categ2's domain are integrated into Categ3's domain as shown in Figure 7.4.

The word, i.e., *girl*, followed by (*A*) in the *A* phrase of the second sentence (55), the word, i.e., *kitchen*, followed by (*G*) in the *G* phrase of (55), and the word, i.e., *go*, followed by (*AC*) in the *AC* phrase of (55) are registered for concepts `girl`, `kitchen`, and `go`, respectively, in Concept-Sound Lexicon. Hence, in this state, no words are stored into Inflection Base.

Because Categ1 was formed in *A* Categorization Base, the entry for *boy*(*A*) in Expansion Base is replaced with the entry for Categ1, and the condition on which Categ1 accompanies function words *does the* is stored into this base in the form of an and/or-tree of depth 1. Rule (Categ1 → does the Categ1) indicates that every member of Categ1 can accompany function words *does the* which it follows. The condition is the one which the condition on which content word *boy(A)* accompanied function words *does the* in the first sentence (54) and the condition on which content word *girl(A)* accompanies function words *does the* in the second sentence (55) are integrated into. BUD considers either that all of the four subconditions in the root node and both of the two subconditions in the left leaf node must be satisfied, or that all of the four subconditions in the root node and both of the two subconditions in the right leaf node must be satisfied, for Categ1 to accompany *does the*. If parameter *depth* = 0, only the root node would be stored here as the condition. The condition on which content word *kitchen(G)* accompanies function words *to the* is also stored into this base in the form of an and/or-tree of depth 0. Note that the A slot in this condition has Categ1 as a part of its value, and that the AC slot has Categ3 as its entire value. If BUD got (55) without (54), the value of the A slot in the condition would be *does the girl(A)*, and the value of the AC slot would be *go(AC)*. Hence, the condition in Figure 7.4 is a generalized condition. It permits an A phrase to be *does the boy(A)*, and an AC phrase to be *kiss(AC)*. Similarly, the condition for *girl(P)* in Figure 7.3 is generalized to the condition in Figure 7.4.

7.2.3. BUD's Behavior in Getting the Third Sample Sentence

Assume that, as shown in Figure 7.5, BUD is given the third sentence (56), its intonation, and its semantic representation as inputs. BUD searches the sentence for content words. As shown in Figure 7.4, Inflection Base is now empty. Hence, BUD finds two words, i.e., *mother* and *father*, which are registered in Concept-Sound Lexicon. Next, BUD searches these two words for ones registered in Subcategorization Base as words which can be main words of sentences. Neither of them is included in Categ3 whose members can be main words of sentences. Hence, BUD cannot find such words.

Sentence 3: The <u>mother</u> <u>kiss</u>iz the <u>father</u>.
            A   AC   P

Intonation: ↓

Semantic Representation:

| A: mother |
| P: father |
| AC: kiss |
| MOOD: declarative |
| TIME: now |

Sound Representation:

| A: mother |
| P: father |
| AC: kiss |
| MOOD: declarative |
| TIME: now |

Synthetic Representation:

| ORDER: A AC P |
| A: the mother(A) |
| P: the father(P) |
| AC: kiss(AC)*iz* |
| INTONATION: ↓ |
| MOOD: declarative |
| TIME: now |

Subcategorization Base:
  Categ3 = (go, kiss)
  Categ3/go - A AC G
  Categ3/kiss - A AC P

Order Management Base:
  A AC P - 2
  A AC G - 1

Inflection Base:
  Categ3/kiss -> Categ3/kiss%*iz*
  Categ3's domain is Subcategorization
  Base and AC.

| ORDER: A AC P |
| A: the mother(A) |
| P: the Categ4 |
| INTONATION: ↓ |
| MOOD: declarative |
| TIME: now |

Expansion Base:
  Categ1 -> does the Categ1
    Categ1's domain is A.

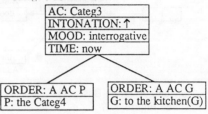

mother(A) -> the mother(A)

| ORDER: A AC P |
| P: the Categ4 |
| AC: Categ3 |
| INTONATION: ↓ |
| MOOD: declarative |
| TIME: now |

kitchen(G) -> to the kitchen(G)
  See Figure 7.4.

Categ4 -> the Categ4
  Categ4's domain is P.

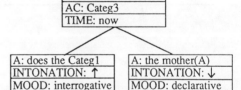

Category Base:
  Categ1 = (boy, girl)
    Categ1's domain is A.
  Categ3 = (go, kiss)
    Categ3's domain is Subcategorization Base
    and AC.
  Categ4 = (father, girl)
    Categ4's domain is P.

Figure 7.5. BUD's Behavior in Getting the Third Sample Sentence

Categorization Bases
A Categorization Base:

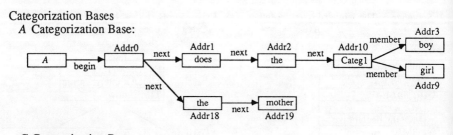

G Categorization Base:
See Figure 7.4.

P Categorization Base:

A C Categorization Base:
See Figure 7.4.

Figure 7.5. BUD's Behavior in Getting the Third Sample Sentence (Continued)

Thus, BUD cannot analyze the third sentence (56) with the knowledge already acquired.

Next, a sound representation is computed from the semantic representation and Concept-Sound Lexicon, and then, a synthetic representation is computed from the sentence, its intonation, and its sound representation in the similar way to the computation of the synthetic representations for both the first sentence (54) and the second sentence (55). The *AC* phrase *kiss*(*AC*)iz indicates that its part, i.e., *kiss*, followed by (*AC*) is the root of the word *kiss*iz, is the value of the *AC* slot in the sound representation, and is registered for some concept in Concept-Sound Lexicon, and that its part, i.e., iz, preceded by (*AC*) is a suffix attached to the root, i.e., *kiss*, of the word.

Hence, the method of obtaining a value of the *AC* slot in the synthetic representation is generalized here from the one mentioned in Section 7.2.1. This value is the words from the word next to *mother* to the word of the *AC* slot, i.e., *kiss*, in the sound representation, or to the word which has the value of the *AC* slot in the sound representation as its root. BUD does not treat endings of inflecting words as independent words. On this point, BUD is dissimilar to CHILD (see Section 4.2). As a result, the value of the *P* slot in the synthetic representation is the words from the word next to the last word of the *AC* phrase to the word of the *P* slot, i.e., *father*, in the sound representation. If there were some words following *father* in the sentence, these words would also be included in the *P* phrase.

In Subcategorization Base, BUD tries to register the value of the *ORDER* slot, i.e., (*A AC P*), in the synthetic representation for the main word, i.e., *kiss*, of the third sentence (56). Note that the main word is not *kiss* iz, but *kiss*. It is the word followed by (*AC*) in the value of the *AC* slot in the synthetic representation (see Section 6.1 (II)). Hence, it is the value of the *AC* slot in the sound representation. Because *kiss* has already been included in Categ3 whose members are considered to be main words of sentences, and because (A AC P) has already been registered for Categ3/*kiss*, nothing is newly stored there.

In Order Management Base, the number of sentences which take an ORDER (A AC P) increases by 1 to 2.

In P Categorization Base, BUD forms a new category Categ4, whose members are *girl* in Addr6 and *father* in Addr20. This category is registered in Category Base with its members and its domain. Note that AC Categorization Base in Figure 7.4 remains unchanged as shown in Figure 7.5. This is because BUD replaces an inflecting word *kiss(AC)iz* in the AC phrase with its original word *kiss(AC)* which is registered for concept kiss in Concept-Sound Lexicon, and because BUD tries to store the resulting phrase into this base. However, *kiss(AC)* has already been stored in this base. Hence, AC Categorization Base in Figure 7.4 remains unchanged.

Now, three categories are stored in Category Base. Although an existing category Categ1 and a new category Categ4 have one common member, i.e., *girl*, as shown in (84), they are not integrated into one category because parameter *integration* = 2.

$$(84)\ |\ \text{Categ1} \cap \text{Categ4}\ | = |\ (\text{girl})\ | = 1$$

Because BUD finds that a word *kiss(AC)iz*, which is not registered for a concept kiss, is used for the concept, it tries to store *kiss(AC)iz* into Inflection Base as another word for the concept. Because *kiss* is included in Categ3, BUD searches Categ3 for a unit which has a subcategorical property that suffix [iz] can be attached to it. Because Categ3 does not have such a unit, a rule (Categ3/*kiss* → Categ3/*kiss*%iz) is newly stored there together with the condition on which suffix [iz] is attached to *kiss(AC)*. This condition is represented as an and/or-tree of depth 0. The left hand, i.e., Categ3/*kiss*, of the rule indicates that *kiss* is a word as a unit of Categ3, and that it is registered for some concept in Concept-Sound Lexicon. The right hand, i.e., Categ3/*kiss*%iz, of the rule indicates that *kiss* can have suffix [iz]. The rule indicates that *kiss* iz corresponds to the concept for which *kiss* is registered in Concept-Sound Lexicon, i.e., kiss. Note that now *kiss* ∈ Categ3 belongs to two units of Categ3, that is, a unit which is constituted by a single word and has a peculiar subcategorical property in Categ3 that it can take an *ORDER* (*A AC P*), and a unit which is also constituted by a single word and has a peculiar subcategorical property in Categ3 that it can have suffix [iz].

In Expansion Base, the value of the *P* slot, i.e., *the girl*(*P*), in the left leaf node of the condition for Categ1 in Figure 7.4 is replaced with *the* Categ4 as shown in Figure 7.5. The condition on which content word *mother*(*A*) accompanies function word *the* is stored into this base in the form of an and/or-tree of depth 0. Note that the value of the *AC* slot in this condition is Categ3 which does not include *kiss* iz. The value reflects the form of the *AC* phrase of the third sentence (56), which was stored into *AC* Categorization Base. Because Categ4 was formed in *P* Categorization Base, the entry for *girl*(*P*) in Expansion Base is replaced with the entry for Categ4, and the condition on which Categ4 accompanies function word *the* is also stored into this base in the form of an and/or-tree of depth 1.

7.2.4. BUD's Behavior in Getting the Fourth Sample Sentence

Assume that, as shown in Figure 7.6, BUD is given the fourth sentence (57), its intonation, and its semantic representation as inputs. BUD searches the sentence for content words. As shown in Figure 7.5, only *kiss*iz is registered in Inflection Base. Hence, BUD finds two words, i.e., *father* and *door*, which are registered in Concept-Sound Lexicon. Next, BUD searches these two words for ones registered in Subcategorization Base as words which can be main words of sentences. Neither of them is included in Categ3 whose

98

Sentence 4: The <u>father</u> <u>open</u>z the <u>door</u>.
            A   AC   P

Intonation: ↓

Semantic Representation:

A: father
P: door
AC: open
MOOD: declarative
TIME: now

Sound Representation:

A: father
P: door
AC: open
MOOD: declarative
TIME: now

Synthetic Representation:

ORDER: A AC P
A: the father(A)
P: the door(P)
AC: open(AC)z
INTONATION: ↓
MOOD: declarative
TIME: now

Subcategorization Base:
  Categ3 = (go, kiss, open)
  Categ3/go - A AC G
  Categ3/Subcateg0 = (kiss, open)
  Categ3/Subcateg0 - A AC P

Order Management Base:
  A AC P - 3
  A AC G - 1

Inflection Base:
  Categ3/kiss -> Categ3/kiss%iz
  Categ3's domain is Subcategorization
  Base and AC.

ORDER: A AC P
A: the Categ5
P: the Categ4
INTONATION: ↓
MOOD: declarative
TIME: now

Inflection Base:
  Categ3/open -> Categ3/open%z
  Categ3's domain is Subcategorization
  Base and AC.

ORDER: A AC P
A: the Categ5
P: the Categ4
INTONATION: ↓
MOOD: declarative
TIME: now

Expansion Base:
  Categ1 -> does the Categ1
  Categ1's domain is A.
  See Figure 7.5.

  Categ5 -> the Categ5
  Categ5's domain is A.

ORDER: A AC P
P: the Categ4
AC: Categ3
INTONATION: ↓
MOOD: declarative
TIME: now

  kitchen(G) -> to the kitchen(G)
  See Figure 7.4.

  Categ4 -> the Categ4
  Categ4's domain is P.

ORDER:A AC P
AC: Categ3
TIME: now

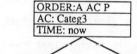

A: does the Categ1		A: the Categ5
INTONATION: ↑		INTONATION:↓
MOOD: interrogative		MOOD: declarative

Category Base:
  Categ1 = (boy, girl)
    Categ1's domain is A.
  Categ3 = (go, kiss, open)
    Categ3's domain is Subcategorization Base
    and AC.
    Categ3/Subcateg0 = (kiss, open)
  Categ4 = (door, father, girl)
    Categ4's domain is P.
  Categ5 = (father, mother)
    Categ5's domain is A.

Figure 7.6. BUD's Behavior in Getting the Fourth Sample Sentence

Categorization Bases
A Categorization Base:

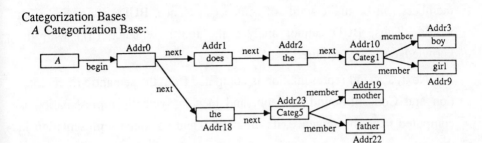

G Categorization Base:
See Figure 7.4.

P Categorization Base:

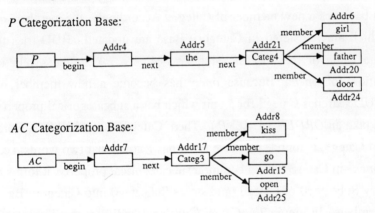

AC Categorization Base:

Figure 7.6. BUD's Behavior in Getting the Fourth Sample Sentence (Continued)

members can be main words of sentences. Hence, BUD cannot find such words. Thus, BUD cannot analyze the fourth sentence (57) with the knowledge already acquired.

Next, a sound representation is computed from the semantic representation and Concept-Sound Lexicon, and then, a synthetic representation is computed from the sentence, its intonation, and its sound representation in the same way as the computation of the synthetic representation for the third sentence (56).

In Subcategorization Base, the main word, i.e., *open*, of the fourth sentence (57) becomes a new member of Categ3. Accordingly, the members of Categ3 which are registered in Category Base are updated. BUD tries to register the value of the *ORDER* slot, i.e., (*A AC P*), in the synthetic representation for *open*. Because *open* has become a new member of Categ3, BUD searches Categ3 for a unit which has a subcategorical property that it can take an *ORDER* (*A AC P*). Then, Categ3/*kiss*, which is a word as a unit of Categ3, is found. Because BUD has learned that two words, i.e., *kiss* and *open*, in Categ3 have a common subcategorical property, it forms a subcategory Subcateg0 of Categ3, and stores Subcateg0 into Category Base with its members. In Figure 7.6, Categ3/Subcateg0 indicates that Subcateg0 is a subcategory as a unit of Categ3. Because Subcateg0 was formed, the entry for Categ3/*kiss* is replaced with the entry for Categ3/Subcateg0. Note that now *kiss* ∈ Categ3 belongs to two units of Categ3, that is, Categ3/Subcateg0 which is a subcategory as a unit of Categ3, and whose members have a common subcategorical property that they can take an *ORDER* (*A AC P*), and Categ3/*kiss* which is a word as a unit of Categ3 and has a peculiar subcategorical property in Categ3 that it can have suffix [iz].

In Order Management Base, the number of sentences which take an *ORDER* (*A AC P*) increases by 1 to 3.

In *A* Categorization Base, BUD forms a new category Categ5 whose members are *mother* in Addr19 and *father* in Addr22. This category is registered in Category Base with its members and its domain.

Now, four categories are stored in Category Base. Although an existing category Categ4 and a new category Categ5 have one member, i.e., *father*, in common as shown in (85), they are not integrated into one category because parameter **integration** = 2.

$$(85) \mid Categ4 \cap Categ5 \mid = \mid (father) \mid = 1$$

In Inflection Base, the value of the *A* slot, i.e., *the mother(A)*, in the condition for Categ3/*kiss* in Figure 7.5 is replaced with *the* Categ5 as shown in Figure 7.6. Because BUD finds that a word *open(AC)z* which is not registered for a concept open is used for the concept, it tries to store *open(AC)z* into Inflection Base as another word for the concept. Because *open* is included in Categ3, BUD searches Categ3 for a unit which has a subcategorical property that suffix [z] can be attached to it. Because Categ3 does not have such a unit, a rule (Categ3/*open* → Categ3/*open%z*) is newly stored there together with the condition on which suffix [z] is attached to *open(AC)*. This condition is represented as an and/or-tree of depth 0.

Because Categ5 was formed in *A* Categorization Base, the entry for *mother(A)* in Expansion Base is replaced with the entry for Categ5, and the condition on which Categ5 accompanies function word *the* is stored into this base in the form of an and/or-tree of depth 0. The condition is represented in this way, although it is the one which the condition on which content word *mother(A)* accompanied function word *the* in the third sentence (56) and the condition on which content word *father(A)* accompanies function word *the* in the fourth sentence (57) are integrated into. This tree consists of only a root node which has six subconditions, and BUD considers that all six subconditions must be satisfied for Categ5 to accompany *the*.

BUD also tries to store into Expansion Base a new condition on which Categ4 accompanies function word *the* in the fourth sentence (57). Then, this base has already had an entry for Categ4. Hence, the condition already stored there and the new condition are integrated into the condition as shown in Figure 7.6. The resulting condition is represented as an and/or-tree of depth 1.

7.2.5. BUD's Behavior in Getting the Fifth Sample Sentence

Assume that, as shown in Figure 7.7, BUD is given the fifth sentence (58), its intonation, and its semantic representation as inputs. BUD searches the sentence for content words. Then, BUD finds two words, i.e., *boy* and *girl*, which are registered in Concept-Sound Lexicon. Next, BUD searches these two words for ones registered in Subcategorization Base as words which can be main words of sentences. Neither of them is included in Categ3 whose members can be main words of sentences. Hence, BUD cannot find such words. Thus, BUD cannot analyze the fifth sentence (58) with the knowledge already acquired.

Next, a sound representation is computed from the semantic representation and Concept-Sound Lexicon, and then, a synthetic representation is computed from the sentence, its intonation, and its sound representation in the same way as the computation of the synthetic representations for the third sentence (56) and for the fourth sentence (57).

In Subcategorization Base, the main word, i.e., *touch*, of the fifth sentence (58) becomes a new member of Categ3. Accordingly, the members of Categ3 which are registered in Category Base are updated. BUD tries to register the value of the *ORDER* slot, i.e., (*A AC P*), in the synthetic representation for *touch*. Because *touch* has become a new member of Categ3, BUD searches Categ3 for a unit which has a subcategorical property that it can take an *ORDER* (*A AC P*). Then, Categ3/Subcateg0, which is a

Sentence 5: The boy touch*iz* the girl.
$\quad\quad\quad\quad\quad\quad\,$ A $\quad$ AC $\quad\quad$ P

Intonation: ↓

Semantic Representation:

| A: boy |
| P: girl |
| AC: touch |
| MOOD: declarative |
| TIME: now |

Sound Representation:

| A: boy |
| P: girl |
| AC: touch |
| MOOD: declarative |
| TIME: now |

Synthetic Representation:

| ORDER: A AC P |
| A: the boy(A) |
| P: the girl(P) |
| AC: touch(AC)*iz* |
| INTONATION: ↓ |
| MOOD: declarative |
| TIME: now |

Subcategorization Base:
Categ3 = (go, kiss, open, touch)
Categ3/go - A AC G

Categ3/Subcateg0 = (kiss, open, touch)
Categ3/Subcateg0 - A AC P

⇓

Categ3/Subcateg2 = (kiss, open, touch)
Categ3/Subcateg2 - A AC P

Order Management Base:
A AC P - 4
A AC G - 1

Inflection Base:
Categ3/Subcateg1 -> Categ3/Subcateg1%*iz*
⇓
Categ3/Subcateg2 -> Categ3/Subcateg2%*iz*
Categ3's domain is Subcategorization
Base and AC.

| ORDER: A AC P |
| A: the Categ5 |
| P: the Categ4 |
| INTONATION: ↓ |
| MOOD: declarative |
| TIME: now |

Inflection Base:
Categ3/open -> Categ3/open%*z*
Categ3's domain is Subcategorization
Base and AC.

✓

| ORDER: A AC P |
| A: the Categ5 |
| P: the Categ4 |
| INTONATION: ↓ |
| MOOD: declarative |
| TIME: now |

Expansion Base:
Categ1 -> does the Categ1
Categ1's domain is A.
See Figure 7.5.

Categ5 -> the Categ5
Categ5's domain is A.
See Figure 7.6.

kitchen(G) -> to the kitchen(G)
See Figure 7.4.

Categ4 -> the Categ4
Categ4's domain is P.
See Figure 7.6.

Category Base:
Categ1 = (boy, girl)
Categ1's domain is A.
Categ3 = (go, kiss, open, touch)
Categ3's domain is Subcategorization Base
and AC.
✓ Categ3/Subcateg0 = (kiss, open, touch)
✓ Categ3/Subcateg1 = (kiss, touch)
Categ3/Subcateg0 and Categ3/Subcateg1 are
integrated into Categ3/Subcateg2
Categ3/Subcateg2 = (kiss, open, touch)
Categ4 = (door, father, girl)
Categ4's domain is P.
Categ5 = (boy, father, mother)
Categ5's domain is A.

Figure 7.7. BUD's Behavior in Getting the Fifth Sample Sentence

104

Categorization Bases
A Categorization Base:

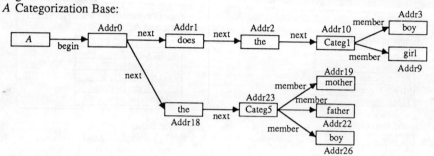

G Categorization Base:
See Figure 7.4.

P Categorization Base:
See Figure 7.6.

AC Categorization Base:

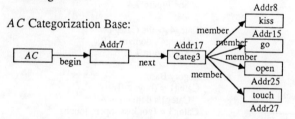

Figure 7.7. BUD's Behavior in Getting the Fifth Sample Sentence (Continued)

subcategory as a unit of Categ3, is found. The word *touch* becomes a new member of Subcateg0, and the members of Subcateg0 which are registered in Category Base are updated.

In Order Management Base, the number of sentences which take an *ORDER* (*A AC P*) increases by 1 to 4.

No new categories are formed in categorization bases.

Because BUD finds that a word *touch*(*AC*)iz, which is not registered for a concept touch, is used for the concept, it tries to store *touch*(*AC*)iz into Inflection Base as another word for the concept. Because *touch* is included in Categ3, BUD searches Categ3 for a unit which has a subcategorical property that suffix [iz] can be attached to it. Then, Categ3/*kiss*, which is a word as a unit of Categ3, is found. Because BUD has learned that two words, i.e., *kiss* and *touch*, in Categ3 have a common subcategorical property, it forms a subcategory Subcateg1 of Categ3, and stores Subcateg1 into Category Base with its members. Because Subcateg1 was formed, the entry for Categ3/*kiss* in Inflection Base is replaced with the entry for Categ3/Subcateg1. In Figure 7.7, the left hand, i.e., Categ3/Subcateg1, of rule (Categ3/Subcateg1 → Categ3/Subcateg1%iz) indicates that Subcateg1 is a subcategory as a unit of Categ3 and that its members are registered for some concepts in Concept-Sound Lexicon. The right hand, i.e., Categ3/Subcateg1%iz, of the rule indicates that every member of Subcateg1 can have suffix [iz]. Now, assume that $X \in$ Subcateg1. The rule indicates that Xiz corresponds to the concept for which X is registered in Concept-Sound Lexicon. The condition on which suffix [iz] is attached to Categ3/Subcateg1 is stored into this base in the form of an and/or-tree of depth 0. Note that it is represented in this way, although it is the condition which the condition on which *kiss* had suffix [iz] in the third sentence (56) and the condition on which *touch* has suffix [iz] in the fifth sentence (58) are integrated into.

Now, two subcategories of Categ3, i.e., Subcateg0 and Subcateg1, are stored in Category Base. The number of words in the intersection of the two subcategories is two, as given by

(86) | Subcateg0 ∩ Subcateg1 | = | (kiss, touch) | = 2.

Because parameter *integration −for −sub** = 2, and because the other condition (i) introduced in Section 6.2 (I) is also satisfied, Subcateg0 and Subcateg1 are integrated into Subcateg2.

(87) Subcateg2 = Subcateg0 ∪ Subcateg1 = (kiss, open, touch)

Hence, the entry for Categ3/Subcateg0 in Subcategorization Base and the entry for Categ3/Subcateg1 in Inflection Base are replaced with Categ3/Subcateg2. Two entries for Categ3/Subcateg0 and Categ3/Subcateg1 are removed from Category Base, and Categ3/Subcateg2 is stored there with its members. Every member in Categ3/Subcateg2 is considered to have both a subcategorical property that it can take an *ORDER* (*A AC P*), and a subcategorical property that it can have suffix [iz].

Now, BUD compares this condition with that on the application of rule (Categ3/*open* → Categ3/*open*%z), because *open* is a member of Categ3/Subcateg2. These two conditions are identical. BUD cannot understand which should be used, *openz* or *openiz*, when the condition is satisfied. This violates the assumption that a form is in one-to-one correspondence with a meaning (see Section 4.3). BUD considers that *openiz* is correct, and that *openz* is incorrect, because rule (Categ3/Subcateg2 → Categ3/Subcateg2%iz) was made more recently than rule (Categ3/*open* → Categ3/*open*%z). Hence, the entry for Categ3/*open* is removed from Inflection Base. Thus, an **overgeneralization** on the application of rule (Categ3/Subcateg2 → Categ3/Subcateg2%iz) has occurred. If the condition on the application of the rule is satisfied, BUD will apply the rule to *open* , to which it should not be applied, that is, BUD will produce *open*iz.

Expansion Base remains unchanged.

7.2.6. BUD's Behavior in Getting the Sixth Sample Sentence

Assume that, as shown in Figure 7.8, BUD is given the sixth sentence (59), its intonation, and its semantic representation as inputs. BUD searches the sentence for content words. Then, BUD finds three words, i.e., *mother*, *touch*, and *boy*, which are registered in Concept-Sound Lexicon. Next, BUD searches these three words for ones registered in Subcategorization Base as words which can be main words of sentences. Then, BUD finds *touch* included in Categ3, whose members can be main words of sentences. Hence, BUD tries to make a possible synthetic representation on the basis of the sentence, its intonation, Concept-Sound Lexicon, and the information stored in the several databases. Figure 7.9 illustrates how to make a possible synthetic representation.

First, BUD fetches subcategorization information of *touch*(AC) ∈ Categ3/Subcateg2 from Subcategorization Base, and gets an *ORDER* (A AC P). The number of content words BUD found in the sentence must equal the number of role names involved by the *ORDER*. Then, both of them are 3. Because the three content words appear in the sentence in the order of *mother*, *touch*, and *boy*, BUD considers that A, AC, and P in the *ORDER* correspond to *mother*, *touch*, and *boy*, respectively.

As shown in Figure 7.7, Inflection Base has an entry for *touch*(AC) ∈ Categ3/Subcateg2, and Expansion Base has an entry for *mother*(A) ∈ Categ5.

BUD does not apply rule (Categ3/Subcateg2 → Categ3/Subcateg2%iz) stored in Inflection Base to *touch*(AC), because content word *touch* which BUD found in the sentence is registered in Concept-Sound Lexicon, and not

108

Sentence 6: Does the <u>mother</u> <u>touch</u> the <u>boy</u>?
          A   AC   P

Intonation: ↑

Semantic Representation:

A: mother
P: boy
AC: touch
MOOD: interrogative
TIME: now

Sound Representation:

A: mother
P: boy
AC: touch
MOOD: interrogative
TIME: now

Synthetic Representation:

ORDER: A AC P	⇒ does A AC P
A: does the mother(A)	⇒ the mother(A)
P: the boy(P)	
AC: touch(AC)	
INTONATION: ↑	
MOOD: interrogative	
TIME: now	

Subcategorization Base:
Categ3 = (go, kiss, open, touch)
Categ3/go - A AC G
Categ3/touch - does A AC P
Categ3/Subcateg2 = (kiss, open, touch)
Categ3/Subcateg2 - A AC P

Order Management Base:
A AC P - 5 ⇒ 4
A AC G - 1
does A AC P - 1

Inflection Base:
Categ3/Subcateg2 -> Categ3/Subcateg2%iz
Categ3's domain is Subcategorization
Base and AC.

ORDER: A AC P
A: the Categ7
P: the Categ7
INTONATION: ↓
MOOD: declarative
TIME: now

Inflection Base:
Categ3/touch -> Categ3/touch%
Categ3's domain is Subcategorization
Base and AC.

ORDER: does A AC P
A: the Categ7
P: the Categ7
INTONATION: ↑
MOOD: interrogative
TIME: now

Expansion Base:
Categ7 -> the Categ7
Categ7's domain is A and P.
for A,

AC: Categ3
TIME: now

INTONATION: ↑		ORDER: A AC P
MOOD: interrogative		P: the Categ7
		INTONATION: ↓
		MOOD: declarative

for P,

A: the Categ7
AC: Categ3
TIME: now

ORDER: does A AC P		ORDER: A AC P
INTONATION: ↑		INTONATION: ↓
MOOD: interrogative		MOOD: declarative

kitchen(G) -> to the kitchen(G)

ORDER: does A AC G
A: the Categ7
AC: Categ3
INTONATION: ↑
MOOD: interrogative
TIME: now

Figure 7.8. BUD's Behavior in Getting the Sixth Sample Sentence

Category Base:
√Categ1 = (boy, girl, mother)
    Categ1's domain is A.
    Categ3 = (go, kiss, open, touch)
    Categ3's domain is Subcategorization Base
    and AC.
    Categ3/Subcateg2 = (kiss, open, touch)
√Categ4 = (boy, door, father, girl)
    Categ4's domain is P.
√Categ5 = (boy, father, mother)
    Categ5's domain is A.
    Categ1 and Categ4 are integrated into Categ6.
√Categ6 = (boy, door, father, girl, mother)
    Categ6's domain is A and P.
    Categ5 and Categ6 are integrated into Categ7.
    Categ7 = (boy, door, father, girl, mother)

Possible Synthetic Representation:

ORDER: A AC P
A: the mother(A)
P: the Categ4
AC: Categ3
INTONATION: ↓
MOOD: declarative
TIME: now

= the *ORDER* (A AC P)
    (Subcategorization Information of
    touch(AC) ∈ Categ3/Subcateg2)

≠ the given intonation: ↑

Figure 7.8. BUD's Behavior in Getting the Sixth Sample Sentence (Continued)

110

Categorization Bases
A Categorization Base:

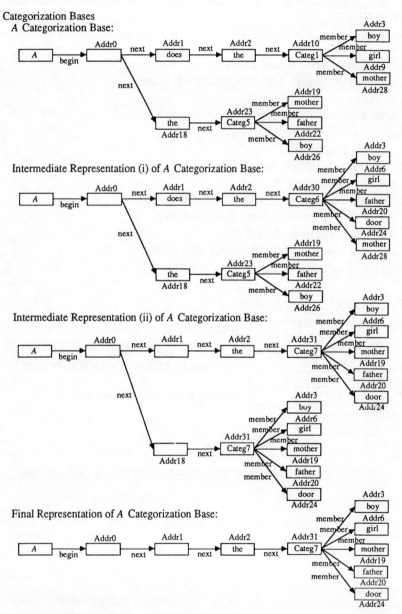

Figure 7.8. BUD's Behavior in Getting the Sixth Sample Sentence (Continued)

Categorization Bases
  G Categorization Base:
    See Figure 7.4.

P Categorization Base

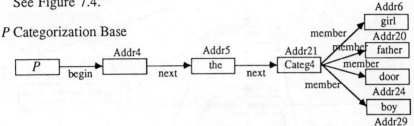

Intermediate Representation of P Categorization Base:

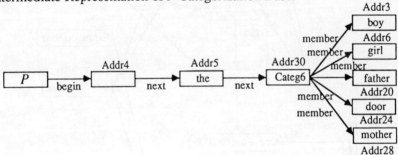

Final Representation of P Categorization Base:

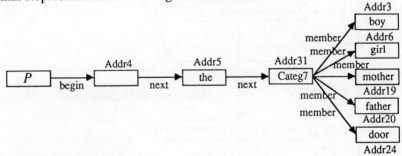

AC Categorization Base:
  See Figure 7.7.

Figure 7.8. BUD's Behavior in Getting the Sixth Sample Sentence (Continued)

112

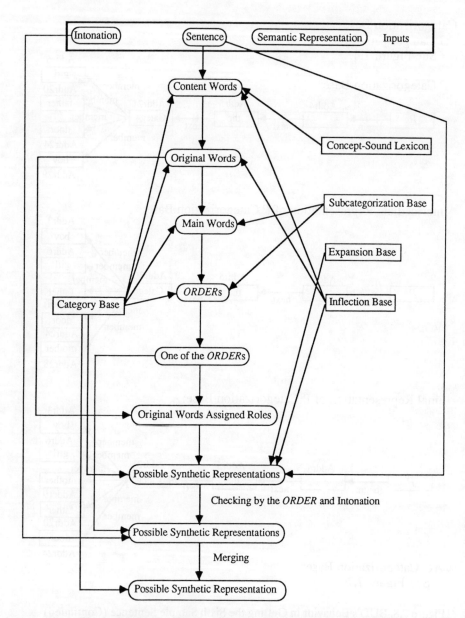

Figure 7.9. How to Make a Possible Synthetic Representation

in Inflection Base.

BUD tries to apply rule (Categ5 › the Categ5) stored in Expansion Base to *mother*(A). Then, *the mother*(A) is made. In fact, the sentence involves *the mother*. If the sentence did not involve *the mother*, BUD would have failed in applying the rule to *mother*(A). As shown in Figure 7.6, the condition on the application of the rule is represented as an and/or-tree of depth 0. Hence, BUD considers that all the six subconditions in the root node must be satisfied in applying the rule to *mother*(A). Thus, a possible synthetic representation is made as shown in Figure 7.8. It can be regarded as a hypothesis BUD makes on the basis of the knowledge already acquired.

BUD checks the possible synthetic representation by the *ORDER* and the intonation given with the sentence as follows. First, BUD examines whether or not the value of the *ORDER* slot in the possible synthetic representation matches the *ORDER* (A AC P). Then, they are the same. Second, BUD examines whether or not the value of the *INTONATION* slot in the possible synthetic representation matches the intonation given with the sentence as an input. Then, this value, $\downarrow$, is different from the given intonation, i.e., $\uparrow$. Thus, BUD has failed in applying the rule to *mother*(A). Hence, the possible synthetic representation is discarded. BUD cannot analyze sentence (59) with the knowledge already acquired.

Now, a sound representation is computed from the semantic representation and Concept-Sound Lexicon, and then, a synthetic representation is computed from the sentence, its intonation, and its sound representation in the same way as the computation of the synthetic representations for the first sentence (54) and for the second sentence (55).

In Subcategorization Base, BUD tries to register the value of the *ORDER* slot, i.e., (A AC P), in the synthetic representation for the main word, i.e., *touch*, of the sixth sentence (59). Because *touch* has already been included in Categ3 whose members can be main words of sentences, and because (*A AC P*) has already been registered for Categ3/Subcateg2 which includes *touch*, nothing is newly stored there.

In Order Management Base, the number of sentences which take an *ORDER* (*A AC P*) increases by 1 to 5.

No new categories are formed in categorization bases.

Now, four categories are stored in Category Base. The number of words in the intersection of Categ1 and Categ4 is two, as given by

(88)| Categ1 ∩ Categ4 | = | (boy, girl) | = 2.

Because parameter *integration* = 2, and because the other condition (i) introduced in Section 6.2 (II) is also satisfied, Categ1 and Categ4 are integrated into Categ6.

(89) Categ6 = Categ1 ∪ Categ4 = (boy, door, father, girl, mother)

BUD updates the contents in *A* Categorization Base and *P* Categorization Base, and thus makes an intermediate representation (i) of *A* Categorization Base, and an intermediate representation of *P* Categorization Base as shown in Figure 7.8.

The number of words in the intersection of Categ5 and Categ6 is three, as given by

(90)| Categ5 ∩ Categ6 | = | (boy, father, mother) | = 3.

Because parameter *integration* = 2, and because the other condition (i) introduced in Section 6.2 (II) is also satisfied, Categ5 and Categ6 are integrated into Categ7.

(91) Categ7 = Categ5 ∪ Categ6 = (boy, door, father, girl, mother)

BUD updates the contents in A Categorization Base and P Categorization Base, and thus makes an intermediate representation (ii) of A Categorization Base, and a final representation of P Categorization Base as shown in Figure 7.8.

Now, every member of Categ7 is considered to have the following three categorical properties:

> (92) In A Categorization Base,
>
>   does the Categ7
>
> (93) In A Categorization Base,
>
>   the Categ7
>
> (94) In P Categorization Base,
>
>   the Categ7

Every member of Categ7 has two categorical properties (92) and (93), related to A Categorization Base. When a category has more than one categorical property related to the same categorization base, such categorical properties are compared with one another. In the above case, properties (92) and (93) are compared with each other. Now, parameter *do−hash−begin* is t, property (92) consists of three words, and property (93) consists of two words. Hence, BUD examines whether or not the last two words in (92) are the same as the two words in (93). If *do-hash-begin* were *nil*, BUD would examine whether or not the first two words in (92) were the same as the two words in (93). Then, they are the same. If they were different, nothing would occur. As a result, the word in (92) which is not included in (93), i.e., *does*, is removed from (92). BUD considers that every member of Categ7 has two categorical properties (93) and (94), and thus makes a final representation of A Categorization Base as shown in Figure 7.8. Note that *boys* in the final representation of A Categorization Base and in the final representation of P Categorization Base have the same address, i.e., Addr3. The same is true of the other members of Categ7, i.e., *girl*, *mother*, *father*, and *door*. This indicates that the five words have two common properties, (93) and (94).

Two entries for Categ1 and Categ4 are removed from Category Base, and Categ6 is stored there with its members and its domain. Then, two entries for Categ5 and Categ6 are also removed from Category Base, and Categ7 is stored there with its members and its domain.

The A phrase of the sixth sentence (59) has not contained *does*, so that the values of the *ORDER* and the A slots in the synthetic representation are updated as shown in Figure 7.8. From now on, when BUD finds an A phrase whose first word is *does*, BUD will remove *does* from the A phrase, and will insert it just before A in the value of the *ORDER* slot in the synthetic representation.

When BUD considered that the value of the *ORDER* slot in the synthetic representation of the sixth sentence (59) was (A AC P), it stored nothing new into Subcategorization Base, and the number of sentences which take an *ORDER* (A AC P) increased by 1 to 5 in Order Management Base. However, now the value is (does A AC P). Hence, in Subcategorization Base, the value is registered for the main word, i.e., *touch*, of the sentence. Categ3's members remain unchanged. In Order Management Base, the number of sentences which take the *ORDER* (A AC P) decreases by 1 to 4, and the number, i.e., 1, of sentences which take the *ORDER* (does A AC P) is newly stored there.

Two matters should be noted here. First, although not (does A AC P) but (A AC P) was registered for the main word, i.e., *kiss*, of the first sentence (54), and although not (does A AC G) but (A AC G) was registered for the main word, i.e., *go*, of the second sentence (55), these (A AC P) and

(*A AC G*) are not changed into (does *A AC P*) and (does *A AC G*), respectively. This is because a synthetic representation of a sentence is a temporal representation (see Section 5.2). The synthetic representations of the first and the second sentences have been lost, and BUD cannot obtain access to them. Second, now *touch* ∈ Categ3 belongs to two units of Categ3, that is, Categ3/Subcateg2 whose members have both a subcategorical property that they can take an *ORDER* (*A AC P*) and a subcategorical property that they can have suffix [iz], and Categ3/*touch* which has a peculiar subcategorical property in Categ3 that it can take an *ORDER* (does *A AC P*).

BUD has already known that *touch(AC)*iz (*touch(AC)* ∈ Categ3/Subcateg2), which is not registered for a concept touch in Concept-Sound Lexicon, can be used for the concept. In the sixth sentence (59), the original word *touch(AC)* is used for the concept. Hence, the original word is stored into Inflection Base with the condition on which it is used (see Section 6.1 (III)). In Figure 7.8, the left hand, i.e., Categ3/*touch*, of rule (Categ3/*touch* → Categ3/*touch*%) indicates that *touch* is a word as a unit of Categ3, and the right hand, i.e., Categ3/*touch*%, of the rule indicates that *touch* can be used without any suffixes. Now, *touch* ∈ Categ3 belongs to three units of Categ3, that is, Categ3/Subcateg2, whose members have both a subcategorical property that they can take an *ORDER* (*A AC P*) and a subcategorical property that they can have suffix [iz], Categ3/*touch*, which has a peculiar subcategorical property in Categ3 that it can take an *ORDER* (does *A AC P*), and Categ3/*touch* which has a peculiar subcategorical property in Categ3 that it can be used without any suffixes.

In Expansion Base, BUD transforms rule (Categ1 → does the Categ1) into rule (Categ1 → the Categ1), updates the conditions on the application of rules (Categ1 → the Categ1), (Categ5 → the Categ5), and (Categ4 → the Categ4), and gains conditions (a), (b), and (c) for the rules as shown in Figure 7.10. The condition on which *mother(A)* ∈ Categ7 accompanies *the* in the A phrase of the sixth sentence (59) is illustrated by (d) in Figure 7.10, and the condition on which $boy(P) \in$ Categ7 accompanies *the* in the P phrase of the sentence is illustrated by (e). Because Categ1 and Categ4 were integrated into Categ6, and because Categ5 and Categ6 were integrated into Categ7, three entries for Categ1, Categ5, and Categ4 are removed from Expansion Base, and the entry for Categ7 is stored there. Because Categ7's domain is A and P, the two conditions, i.e., that on which Categ7 accompanies *the* in A phrases and that on which Categ7 accompanies *the* in P phrases, are stored there. The former condition is the one which three conditions (a), (b), and (d) are integrated into, and is illustrated by (f) in Figure 7.10. The latter condition is the one which two conditions (c) and (e) are integrated into, and is illustrated by (h) in Figure 7.10. Both of these conditions are represented as and/or-trees of depth 1.

Now we explain how to make an and/or-tree (f) of depth 1 from (a), (b), and (d). First, because (a) is represented as an and/or-tree of depth 1, and because it has two leaf nodes, it is dissolved into two conditions (a1) and (a2). Then, all of the four conditions (a1), (a2), (b), and (d) are represented as and/or-trees of depth 0. Next, BUD finds two subconditions, i.e., $(AC:$ Categ3$)$ and $(TIME:$ now$)$, which are common to the four conditions. These two subconditions constitute the root node of (f). Next, BUD makes (a1′), (a2′), (b′), and (d′) by removing the two subconditions from (a1), (a2), (b), and (d), respectively. BUD searches the four resulting conditions for subconditions contained in three of the resulting conditions. Then, BUD finds three subconditions, i.e., $(P:$ the Categ7$)$, $(INTONATION: \uparrow)$, and $(MOOD:$ interrogative$)$. Next, BUD finds that two subconditions, i.e., $(INTONATION: \uparrow)$ and $(MOOD:$ interrogative$)$, are contained in three common conditions, i.e., (a1′), (a2′), and (d′). Thus, these two subconditions constitute the left leaf node. The right leaf node is determined as (b′), which contains neither of the two subconditions. Because *depth* $= 1$, condition (f) made

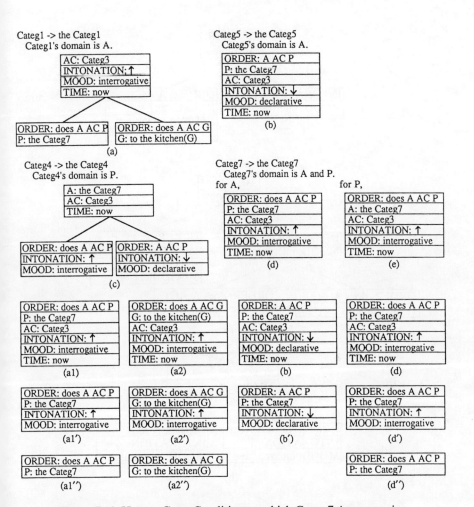

Figure 7.10. How to Get a Condition on which Categ 7 Accompanies *the* in *A* Phrases

120

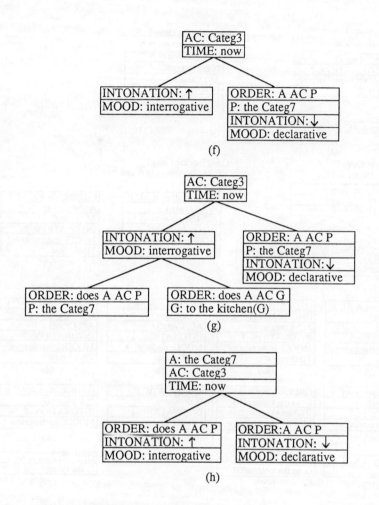

Figure 7.10. How to Get a Condition on which Categ 7 Accompanies
the in *A* Phrases (Continued)

in this way is determined as the condition on which Categ7 accompanies *the* in *A* phrases.

If *depth* $\geq$ 2, BUD would continue making an and/or-tree (g). BUD makes (a1″), (a2″), and (d″) by removing these two subconditions from (a1′), (a2′), and (d′), respectively. BUD searches the three resulting conditions for subconditions contained in two of the resulting conditions. Then, BUD finds two subconditions, i.e., (*ORDER*: does *A AC P*) and (*P*: the Categ7). Next, BUD finds that the two subconditions are contained in two common conditions, i.e., (a1″) and (d″). Thus, these two subconditions constitute the left-most leaf node of (g). As a result, the right leaf node which is a daughter of the left daughter node of the root node is determined as (a2″), which contains neither of these two subconditions. Thus, condition (g), which is represented as an and/or-tree of depth 2, would be determined as the condition on which Categ7 accompanies *the* in *A* phrases.

BUD also updates the condition on which content word *kitchen(G)* accompanies function words *to the* as shown in Figure 7.8.

7.2.7. BUD's Behavior in Getting the Seventh Sample Sentence

Assume that, as shown in Figure 7.11, BUD is given the seventh sentence (60), its intonation, and its semantic representation as inputs. BUD searches the sentence for content words. Then, BUD finds three words, i.e., *father*, *touch*, and *mother*, which are registered in Concept-Sound Lexicon. The word *touch* is also registered in Inflection Base. Next, BUD searches these three words for ones registered in Subcategorization Base as words which can be main words of sentences. Then, BUD finds *touch* included in Categ3, whose members can be main words of sentences. Hence, BUD tries to make a possible synthetic representation on the basis of the sentence, its intonation, Concept-Sound Lexicon, and the information stored in the several databases.

122

Sentence 7: Does the <u>father</u> <u>touch</u> the <u>mother</u>?
                    A   AC   P

Intonation: ↑

Semantic Representation:

| A: father |
| P: mother |
| AC: touch |
| MOOD: interrogative |
| TIME: now |

Sound Representation:

| A: father |
| P: mother |
| AC: touch |
| MOOD: interrogative |
| TIME: now |

Synthetic Representation:

| ORDER: does A AC P |
| A: the father(A) |
| P: the mother(P) |
| AC: touch(AC) |
| INTONATION: ↑ |
| MOOD: interrogative |
| TIME: now |

Subcategorization Base:
  Categ3 = (go, kiss, open, touch)
  Categ3/go - A AC G
  Categ3/touch - does A AC P
  Categ3/Subcateg2 = (kiss, open, touch)
  Categ3/Subcateg2 - A AC P

Order Management Base:
  A AC P - 4
  does A AC P - 2
  A AC G - 1

Categorization Bases:
  See Figure 7.8.

Inflection Base:
  Categ3/Subcateg2 -> Categ3/Subcateg2%*iz*
  Categ3's domain is Subcategorization
  Base and AC.

| ORDER: A AC P |
| A: the Categ7 |
| P: the Categ7 |
| INTONATION: ↓ |
| MOOD: declarative |
| TIME: now |

Inflection Base:
  Categ3/touch -> Categ3/touch%
  Categ3's domain is Subcategorization
  Base and AC.

| ORDER: does A AC P |
| A: the Categ7 |
| P: the Categ7 |
| INTONATION: ↑ |
| MOOD: interrogative |
| TIME: now |

Expansion Base:
  Categ7 -> the Categ7
  Categ7's domain is A and P.
  for A,

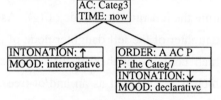

  for P,

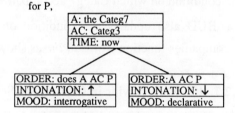

  kitchen(G) -> to the kitchen(G)

| ORDER: does A AC G |
| A: the Categ7 |
| AC: Categ3 |
| INTONATION: ↑ |
| MOOD: interrogative |
| TIME: now |

Category Base:
  Categ3 = (go, kiss, open, touch)
    Categ3's domain is Subcategorization Base
    and AC.
    Categ3/Subcateg2 = (kiss, open, touch)
  Categ7 = (boy, door, father, girl, mother)
    Categ7's domain is A and P.

Figure 7.11. BUD's Behavior in Getting the Seventh Sample Sentence

Five Possible Synthetic Representations:

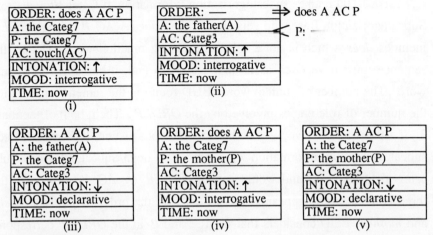

ORDER: does A AC P
A: the Categ7
P: the Categ7
AC: touch(AC)
INTONATION: ↑
MOOD: interrogative
TIME: now

(i)

ORDER: —	⟹ does A AC P
A: the father(A)	⟸ P: —
AC: Categ3	
INTONATION: ↑	
MOOD: interrogative	
TIME: now	

(ii)

ORDER: A AC P
A: the father(A)
P: the Categ7
AC: Categ3
INTONATION: ↓
MOOD: declarative
TIME: now

(iii)

ORDER: does A AC P
A: the Categ7
P: the mother(P)
AC: Categ3
INTONATION: ↑
MOOD: interrogative
TIME: now

(iv)

ORDER: A AC P
A: the Categ7
P: the mother(P)
AC: Categ3
INTONATION: ↓
MOOD: declarative
TIME: now

(v)

Possible synthetic representations (i), (ii), and (iv) are merged into (vi).

ORDER: does A AC P
A: the father(A)
P: the mother(P)
AC: touch(AC)
INTONATION: ↑
MOOD: interrogative
TIME: now

(vi)

Figure 7.11. BUD's Behavior in Getting the Seventh Sample Sentence (Continued)

First, BUD fetches subcategorization information of Categ3/*touch* from Subcategorization Base, and gets an *ORDER* (does *A AC P*). The *ORDER* includes *does* which is not a role name, but a function word. Hence, the sentence must have *does* as its first word. In fact, it has *does* as its first word. The number of content words BUD found in the sentence must equal the number of role names involved by the *ORDER*. Then, both of them are 3. If either of the above two conditions were not satisfied, BUD would fetch subcategorization information of *touch* ∈ Categ3/Subcateg2 from Subcategorization Base, and would get an *ORDER* (*A AC P*). Because the three content words appear in the sentence in the order of *father*, *touch*, and *mother*, BUD considers that *A*, *AC*, and *P* in the *ORDER* correspond to *father*, *touch*, and *mother*, respectively.

As shown in Figure 7.8, Inflection Base has two entries for *touch*(*AC*), and Expansion Base has an entry for *father*(*A*) ∈ Categ7 and an entry for *mother*(*P*) ∈ Categ7.

BUD does not apply rule (Categ3/Subcateg2 → Categ3/Subcateg2%iz) stored in Inflection Base to *touch*(*AC*), because BUD did not get *touch* by applying rule (Categ3/Subcateg2%iz ← Categ3/Subcateg2) to *touch*iz.

BUD tries to apply rule (Categ3/*touch* → Categ3/*touch*%) stored in Inflection Base to *touch*(*AC*), because content word *touch* which BUD found in the sentence is registered not only in Concept-Sound Lexicon, but also in Inflection Base. Then, *touch*(*AC*) is made. As shown in Figure 7.8, the condition on the application of the rule is represented as an and/or-tree of depth 0. Hence, BUD considers that all the six subconditions in the root node must be satisfied in applying the rule to *touch*(*AC*). Thus, a possible synthetic representation (i) is made as shown in Figure 7.11.

Next, BUD tries to apply rule (Categ7 → the Categ7) stored in Expansion Base to *father*(*A*). Then, *the father*(*A*) is made. In fact, the sentence involves *the father*. As shown in Figure 7.8, the condition on which Categ7 accompanies *the* in *A* phrases is represented as an and/or-tree of depth 1. Hence, in applying the rule to *father(A)*, BUD considers either that both of the two subconditions in the root node and both of the two subconditions in the left leaf node must be satisfied, or that both of the two subconditions in the root node and all of the four subconditions in the right leaf node must be satisfied. Thus, two possible synthetic representations (ii) and (iii) are made as shown in Figure 7.11. In (ii), "—" is a wild card which matches any value.

Next, BUD tries to apply rule (Categ7 → the Categ7) stored in Expansion Base to *mother(P)*. Then, *the mother(P)* is made. In fact, the sentence involves *the mother*. As shown in Figure 7.8, the condition on which Categ7 accompanies *the* in *P* phrases is represented as an and/or-tree of depth 1. Hence, in applying the rule to *mother(P)*, BUD considers either that all of the three subconditions in the root node and all of the three subconditions in the left leaf node must be satisfied, or that all of the three subconditions in the root node and all of the three subconditions in the right leaf node must be satisfied. Thus, two possible synthetic representations (iv) and (v) are made as shown in Figure 7.11.

Now, five possible synthetic representations have been made. BUD searches them for ones which satisfy the following two conditions:

- The value of the *ORDER* slot in a possible synthetic representation must match the *ORDER* (does *A AC P*).
- The value of the *INTONATION* slot in a possible synthetic representation must match the intonation given with the sentence as an input, i.e., ↑.

Then, (i), (ii), and (iv) satisfy the above conditions. The remaining possible synthetic representations, i.e., (iii) and (v), are discarded. Two matters should be noted here. First, the value of the *ORDER* slot in (ii) matches the *ORDER* (does *A AC P*), because it is a wild card. The wild card is replaced with the *ORDER* (does *A AC P*). Second, the set of the role names contained in the value of the *ORDER* slot in a possible synthetic representation must be the same as the set of role names (slots) contained in the possible synthetic representation. Possible synthetic representations (i) and (iv) satisfy this condition, but (ii) does not. Hence, a *P* slot which has a wild card as its value is added to (ii).

Next, in (i), which was made on the basis of the condition on the application of rule (Categ3/*touch* → Categ3/*touch*%), BUD searches the role slots for ones whose values are constituted by more than one word. Then, BUD finds the *A* and the *P* slots. Because the value of the *A* slot in (i) is *the* Categ7, BUD searches (ii) and (iv) for ones which were made on the basis of the condition on which Categ7 accompanies *the* in *A* phrases. Then, BUD finds (ii). Because the value of the *P* slot in (i) is *the* Categ7, BUD examines whether or not the remaining possible synthetic representation, i.e., (iv), was made on the basis of the condition on which Categ7 accompanies *the* in *P* phrases. In fact, (iv) was made on the basis of that condition. Hence, BUD tries to merge (i), (ii), and (iv) into (vi).

First, (i), (ii), and (iv) have a common value for each of the *ORDER*, the *INTONATION*, the *MOOD*, and the *TIME* slots. Hence, the values of the four slots in (vi) are determined as those values.

Second, by comparing the values of the *A* slots in (i), (ii), and (iv), BUD examines whether or not Categ7 contains *father*(*A*). Because Categ7 contains *father*(*A*), the value of the *A* slot in (vi) is determined as *the father*(*A*).

Third, by comparing the values of the *P* slots in (i), (ii), and (iv), BUD examines whether or not Categ7 contains *mother*(*P*). Because Categ7 contains *mother*(*P*), the value of the *P* slot in (vi) is determined as *the mother*(*P*).

Finally, by comparing the values of the *AC* slots in (i), (ii), and (iv), BUD examines whether or not Categ3 contains *touch*(*AC*). Because Categ3 contains *touch*(*AC*), the value of the *AC* slot in (vi) is determined as *touch*(*AC*).

Thus, BUD has succeeded in merging (i), (ii), and (iv) into (vi). Hence, (i), (ii), and (iv) are discarded.

Now, BUD computes a sound representation from the semantic representation and Concept-Sound Lexicon, and then, computes a synthetic representation from the sentence, its intonation, and its sound representation in the similar way to the computation of the synthetic representation for the sixth sentence (59). Next, BUD examines whether or not possible synthetic representation (vi) matches the synthetic representation. In this case, they are completely the same. Thus, BUD can analyze the sentence which it has never heard without any reference to the semantic representation given with it as an input, that is, BUD can analyze it with the knowledge already acquired. At the same time, BUD has succeeded in applying rule (Categ3/*touch* → Categ3/*touch%*) to *touch*(*AC*), in applying rule (Categ7 → the Categ7) to *father*(*A*), and in applying rule (Categ7 → the Categ7) to *mother*(*P*). This is because possible synthetic representation (vi) is the one which possible synthetic representation (i) which was made on the basis of the condition on the application of rule (Categ3/*touch* → Categ3/*touch%*), possible synthetic representation (ii) which was made on the basis of the condition on which Categ7 accompanies *the* in *A* phrases, and possible synthetic representation (iv) which was made on the basis of the condition on which Categ7 accompanies *the* in *P* phrases are merged into. From the inputs, i.e., the seventh sentence (60), its intonation, and its semantic representation, BUD learns nothing except that the number of sentences which take an *ORDER* (does *A AC P*) increases by 1 to 2 in Order Management Base.

If possible synthetic representation (vi) did not match the synthetic representation, BUD would fetch subcategorization information of *touch* ∈ Categ3/Subcateg2 from Subcategorization Base, and get an *ORDER* (*A AC P*). Then, BUD would perform the above steps again. If BUD could not make any possible synthetic representations or if the resulting possible synthetic representation did not match the synthetic representation, BUD would find that it could not analyze the sentence with the knowledge already acquired. Then, BUD would learn the syntax of English, inflection of words, and so on on the basis of the synthetic representation.

7.2.8. BUD's Behavior in Getting the Eighth Sample Sentence

Assume that, as shown in Figure 7.12, BUD is given the eighth sentence (61), which contains an unknown content word *cat*, its intonation, and its semantic representation as inputs. BUD searches the sentence for content words. Then, BUD finds a word *touchiz* (*touch* ∈ Categ3/Subcateg2) which is registered in Inflection Base, and a word *girl* which is registered in Concept-Sound Lexicon. Hence, BUD applies rule (Categ3/Subcateg2%iz ← Categ3/Subcateg2) stored in Inflection Base to *touchiz*, and gets its original word registered in Concept-Sound Lexicon, i.e., *touch*. Next, BUD searches the two words *touch* and *girl* for ones registered in Subcategorization Base as words which can be main words of sentences. Then, BUD finds *touch* included in Categ3, whose members can be main words of sentences. Hence, BUD tries to make a possible synthetic representation on the basis of the sentence, its intonation, Concept-Sound Lexicon, and the information stored in the several databases.

First, BUD fetches subcategorization information of Categ3/*touch* from Subcategorization Base, and gets an *ORDER* (does *A AC P*). However, the

Sentence 8: The cat touch*iz* the girl.
$\quad\quad\quad\quad\quad\quad\underline{}$
$\quad\quad\quad\quad\quad\quad\;\,AC\quad\quad\;$P

Intonation: ↓

Semantic Representation:

A: cat
P: girl
AC: touch
MOOD: declarative
TIME: now

Sound Representation:

A: —— ⇒ cat
P: girl
AC: touch
MOOD: declarative
TIME: now

Synthetic Representation:

ORDER: A AC P
A: the cat(A)
P: the girl(P)
AC: touch(AC)*iz*
INTONATION: ↓
MOOD: declarative
TIME: now

Subcategorization Base:
Categ3 = (go, kiss, open, touch)
Categ3/go - A AC G
Categ3/touch - does A AC P
Categ3/Subcateg2 = (kiss, open, touch)
Categ3/Subcateg2 - A AC P

Order Management Base:
A AC P - 5
does A AC P - 2
A AC G - 1

Inflection Base:
Categ3/Subcateg2 -> Categ3/Subcateg2%*iz*
Categ3's Domain is Subcategorization
Base and AC.

ORDER: A AC P
A: the Categ7
P: the Categ7
INTONATION: ↓
MOOD: declarative
TIME: now

Inflection Base:
Categ3/touch -> Categ3/touch%
Categ3's domain is Subcategorization
Base and AC.

ORDER: does A AC P
A: the Categ7
P: the Categ7
INTONATION: ↑
MOOD: interrogative
TIME: now

Expansion Base:
Categ7 -> the Categ7
Categ7's domain is A and P.
for A,

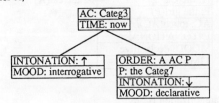

for P,

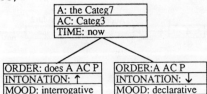

kitchen(G) -> to the kitchen(G)

ORDER: does A AC G
A: the Categ7
AC: Categ3
INTONATION: ↑
MOOD: interrogative
TIME: now

Category Base:
Categ3 = (go, kiss, open, touch)
Categ3's domain is Subcategorization Base
and AC.
Categ3/Subcateg2 = (kiss, open, touch)
Categ7 = (boy, cat, door, father, girl, mother)
Categ7's domain is A and P.

Concept-Sound Lexicon
See Section 7.2.
cat - cat

Figure 7.12. BUD's Behavior in Getting the Eighth Sample Sentence

130

Three Possible Synthetic Representations:

ORDER: A AC P
A: the Categ7
P: the Categ7
AC: touch(AC)iz
INTONATION: ↓
MOOD: declarative
TIME: now

(i)

ORDER: does A AC P
A: the Categ7
P: the girl(P)
AC: Categ3
INTONATION: ↑
MOOD: interrogative
TIME: now

(ii)

ORDER: A AC P
A: the Categ7
P: the girl(P)
AC: Categ3
INTONATION: ↓
MOOD: declarative
TIME: now

(iii)

Possible synthetic representations (i) and (iii) are merged into (iv).

ORDER: does A AC P
A: the Categ7   ⟹   the cat(A)
P: the girl(P)
AC: touch(AC)iz
INTONATION: ↓
MOOD: declarative
TIME: now

(iv)

Categorization Bases
  A Categorization Base:

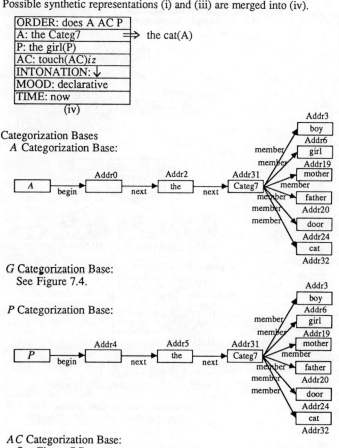

G Categorization Base:
  See Figure 7.4.

P Categorization Base:

A C Categorization Base:
  See Figure 7.7

Figure 7.12. BUD's Behavior in Getting the Eighth Sample Sentence (Continued)

sentence does not have *does* as its first word. Hence, the *ORDER* is discarded. Next, BUD fetches subcategorization information of *touch* ∈ Categ3/Subcateg2 from Subcategorization Base, and gets an *ORDER* (*A AC P*). The number of content words BUD found in the sentence, i.e., 2, does not equal the number of role names contained in the *ORDER*, i.e., 3. Hence, the *ORDER* is also discarded. Thus, BUD cannot analyze the eighth sentence (61) with the knowledge already acquired.

Now, a sound representation is computed from the semantic representation and Concept-Sound Lexicon. Note that the *A* slot of the sound representation has a wild card as its value, because Concept-Sound Lexicon does not have an entry for concept cat. In case that some of the values of the role slots in the sound representation are wild cards, BUD tries to compute a synthetic representation from the sentence, its intonation, its sound representation, and the information stored in the several databases.

First, BUD fetches subcategorization information of Categ3/*touch* from Subcategorization Base, and gets an *ORDER* (does *A AC P*). However, the sentence does not have *does* as its first word. Hence, the *ORDER* is discarded. Next, BUD fetches subcategorization information of *touch* ∈ Categ3/Subcateg2 from Subcategorization Base, and gets an *ORDER* (*A AC P*). The set of role names (slots) contained in the sound representation must be the same as the set of role names contained in the *ORDER*. Then, they are the same. If this condition were not satisfied, BUD would not be able to analyze the sentence, and would ignore it.

As shown in Figure 7.11, Inflection Base has two entries for *touch(AC)*, and Expansion Base has an entry for *girl(P)* ∈ Categ7.

BUD tries to apply rule (Categ3/Subcateg2 → Categ3/Subcateg2%iz) stored in Inflection Base to *touch(AC)*. Then, *touch(AC)*iz is made. In fact, the sentence contains *touch*iz. As shown in Figure 7.11, the condition on the application of the rule is represented as an and/or-tree of depth 0. Thus, a possible synthetic representation (i) is made as shown in Figure 7.12.

Next, BUD tries to apply rule (Categ3/*touch* → Categ3/*touch%*) stored in Inflection Base to *touch*(*AC*). Then, *touch*(*AC*) is made. However, the sentence does not contain *touch* as a word. Hence, BUD has failed in applying the rule to *touch*(*AC*).

Next, BUD tries to apply rule (Categ7 → the Categ7) stored in Expansion Base to *girl*(*P*). Then, *the girl*(*P*) is made. In fact, the sentence involves *the girl*. As shown in Figure 7.11, the condition on the application of the rule is represented as an and/or-tree of depth 1. Thus, two possible synthetic representations (ii) and (iii) are made as shown in Figure 7.12.

Now, three possible synthetic representations have been made. BUD searches them for ones which satisfy the following four conditions:

The value of the *ORDER* slot in a possible synthetic representation must match the *ORDER* (*A AC P*).

· The value of the *INTONATION* slot in a possible synthetic representation must match the intonation given with the sentence as an input, i.e., ↓.

· The value of the *MOOD* slot in a possible synthetic representation must match the value of that slot in the sound representation.

· The value of the *TIME* slot in a possible synthetic representation must match the value of that slot in the sound representation.

Then, (i) and (iii) satisfy the above conditions. The remaining possible synthetic representation, i.e., (ii), is discarded.

Next, in (i), which was made on the basis of the condition on the application of rule (Categ3/Subcateg2 → Categ3/Subcateg2%iz), BUD searches the role slots for the ones whose values are constituted by more than one word. Then, BUD finds the *A* and the *P* slots, both of which have *the*

Categ7 as their values. Because (iii) was made on the basis of the condition on which Categ7 accompanies *the* in *P* phrases, BUD tries to merge (i) and (iii) into (iv).

First, (i) and (iii) have a common value for each of the *ORDER*, the *A*, the *INTONATION*, the *MOOD*, and the *TIME* slots. Hence, the values of these five slots in (iv) are determined as those values.

Second, by comparing the values of the *P* slots in (i) and (iii), BUD examines whether or not Categ7 contains *girl(P)*. Because Categ7 contains *girl(P)*, the value of the *P* slot in (iv) is determined as *the girl(P)*.

Finally, by comparing the values of the *AC* slots in (i) and (iii), BUD examines whether or not Categ3 contains *touch(AC)*. Note that BUD does not examine whether or not Categ3 contains *touch(AC)*iz. This is because categories are constituted by words registered in Concept-Sound Lexicon (see Section 6.1 (I) and Section 7.2.3). Because Categ3 contains *touch(AC)*, the value of the *AC* slot in (iv) is determined as *touch(AC)*iz.

Thus, BUD has succeeded in merging (i) and (iii) into (iv). Hence, (i) and (iii) are discarded.

Now, BUD replaces each role name involved by the value of the *ORDER* slot in (iv) with the value of the corresponding role slot in (iv), and obtains a sequence of words (the Categ7 *touch(AC)*iz the *girl(P)*). By comparing the resulting sequence of words with the eighth sentence (61), BUD infers that *cat* should be a member of Categ7. Then, BUD replaces Categ7 in the value of the *A* slot in (iv) with *cat(A)*. Resulting possible synthetic representation (iv) does not have any indefinite parts, that is, no slots in (iv) have wild cards as their values, and no role slots in (iv) have categories as parts of their values. Hence, (iv) is determined as a synthetic representation of the eighth sentence (61).

Next, the wild card in the A slot of the sound representation is replaced with *cat*. By comparing the values of the A slots in the sound representation and the semantic representation, BUD determines the meaning of the unknown word *cat* as `cat`. Then, a new pair comprising concept `cat` and sound *cat* is registered in Concept-Sound Lexicon. Figure 7.13 illustrates how to learn the meaning of an unknown word.

In Order Management Base, the number of sentences which take an *ORDER* $(A\ AC\ P)$ increases by 1 to 5.

In A Categorization Base and P Categorization Base, *cat* becomes a new member of Categ7. Members of Categ7 have two common categorical properties, that is, a property on their positions in A phrases, and a property on their positions in P phrases. For *cat* to become a new member of Categ7, it need not be guaranteed to have both of the properties, but it must have at least one of the properties (see Section 6.2 (II)). The word *cat* has the former property of Categ7. Accordingly, the members of Categ7 registered in Category Base are updated.

The other databases remain unchanged.

7.2.9. BUD's Behavior in Getting the Ninth Sample Sentence

Assume that, as shown in Figure 7.14, BUD is given the ninth sentence (62), its intonation, and its semantic representation as inputs. BUD searches the sentence for content words. BUD finds two words, i.e., *boy* and *chair*, which are registered in Concept-Sound Lexicon. Next, BUD searches these two words for ones registered in Subcategorization Base as words which can be main words of sentences. Neither of them is included in Categ3, whose members can be main words of sentences. Hence, BUD cannot find such words. Thus, BUD cannot analyze the ninth sentence (62) with the knowledge already acquired.

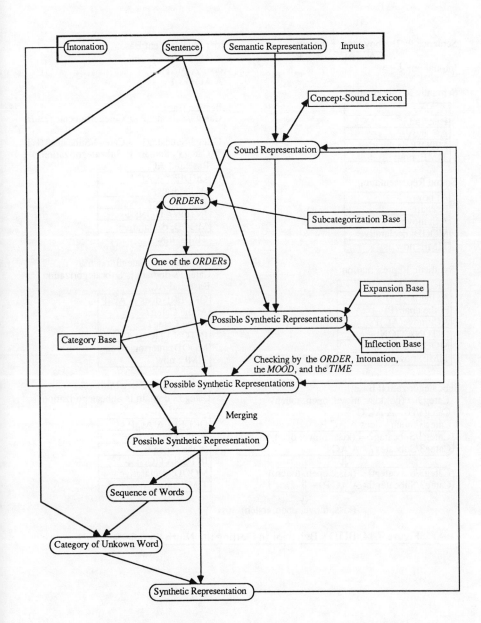

Figure 7.13. How to Learn the Meaning of an Unknown Word

Sentence 9: The boy movez the chair.
        A   AC   P

Intonation: ↓

Semantic Representation:

A: boy
P: chair
AC: move
MOOD: declarative
TIME: now

Sound Representation:

A: boy
P: chair
AC: move
MOOD: declarative
TIME: now

Synthetic Representation:

ORDER: A AC P
A: the boy(A)
P: the chair(P)
AC: move(AC)z
INTONATION:↓
MOOD: declarative
TIME: now

Subcategorization Base:
  Categ3 = (go, kiss, move, open, touch)
  Categ3/go - A AC G
  Categ3/touch - does A AC P
  Categ3/Subcateg2 = (kiss, move, open, touch)
  Categ3/Subcateg2 - A AC P

  Categ3/Subcateg0 = (kiss, open, touch)
  Categ3/Subcateg0 - A AC P

                  ↓
         (kiss, move, open, touch)

Order Management Base:
  A AC P - 6
  does A AC P - 2
  A AC G - 1

Inflection Base:
  Categ3/Subcateg2 -> Categ3/Subcateg2%iz
                  ⇓
  Categ3/Subcateg1 -> Categ3/Subcateg1%iz
  Categ3's domain is Subcategorization
  Base and AC.

ORDER: A AC P
A: the Categ7
P: the Categ7
INTONATION: ↓
MOOD: declarative
TIME: now

Categ3/touch -> Categ3/touch%
  Categ3's domain is Subcategorization
  Base and AC.

ORDER: does A AC P
A: the Categ7
P: the Categ7
INTONATION: ↑
MOOD: interrogative
TIME: now

Categ3/move -> Categ3/move%z
  Categ3's domain is Subcategorization
  Base and AC.

ORDER: A AC P
A: the Categ7
P: the Categ7
INTONATION: ↓
MOOD: declarative
TIME: now

Figure 7.14. BUD's Behavior in Getting the Ninth Sample Sentence

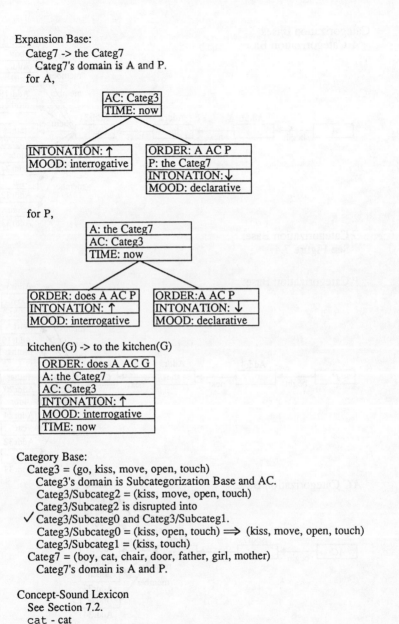

Expansion Base:
  Categ7 -> the Categ7
    Categ7's domain is A and P.
  for A,

```
AC: Categ3
TIME: now
```

```
INTONATION: ↑              ORDER: A AC P
MOOD: interrogative        P: the Categ7
                           INTONATION: ↓
                           MOOD: declarative
```

  for P,

```
A: the Categ7
AC: Categ3
TIME: now
```

```
ORDER: does A AC P         ORDER: A AC P
INTONATION: ↑              INTONATION: ↓
MOOD: interrogative        MOOD: declarative
```

  kitchen(G) -> to the kitchen(G)

```
ORDER: does A AC G
A: the Categ7
AC: Categ3
INTONATION: ↑
MOOD: interrogative
TIME: now
```

Category Base:
  Categ3 = (go, kiss, move, open, touch)
    Categ3's domain is Subcategorization Base and AC.
    Categ3/Subcateg2 = (kiss, move, open, touch)
    Categ3/Subcateg2 is disrupted into
  ✓ Categ3/Subcateg0 and Categ3/Subcateg1.
    Categ3/Subcateg0 = (kiss, open, touch) ⟹ (kiss, move, open, touch)
    Categ3/Subcateg1 = (kiss, touch)
  Categ7 = (boy, cat, chair, door, father, girl, mother)
    Categ7's domain is A and P.

Concept-Sound Lexicon
  See Section 7.2.
  cat - cat

Figure 7.14. BUD's Behavior in Getting the Ninth Sample Sentence (Continued)

138

Categorization Bases
  A Categorization Base:

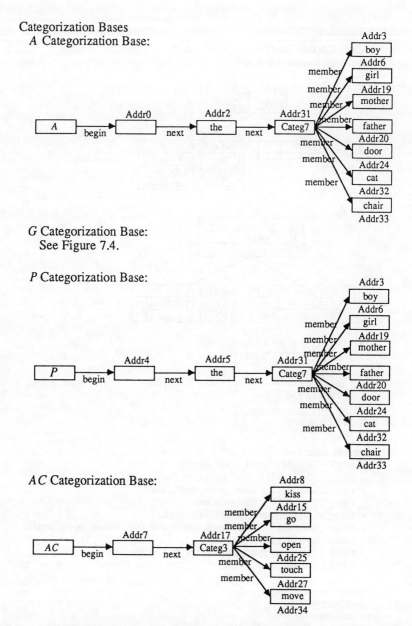

G Categorization Base:
  See Figure 7.4.

P Categorization Base:

AC Categorization Base:

Figure 7.14. BUD's Behavior in Getting the Ninth Sample Sentence (Continued)

Next, a sound representation is computed from the semantic representation and Concept-Sound Lexicon, and then, a synthetic representation is computed from the sentence, its intonation, and its sound representation in the same way to the computation of the synthetic representation for the fifth sentence (58).

In Subcategorization Base, the main word, i.e., *move*, of the ninth sentence (62) becomes a new member of Categ3. Accordingly, the members of Categ3 which are registered in Category Base are updated. BUD tries to register the value of the *ORDER* slot, i.e., (*A AC P*), in the synthetic representation for *move*. Because *move* has become a new member of Categ3, BUD searches Categ3 for a unit which has a subcategorical property that it can take an *ORDER* (*A AC P*). Then, Categ3/Subcateg2, which is a subcategory as a unit of Categ3, is found. Hence, *move* becomes a new member of Categ3/Subcateg2. Accordingly, the members of Categ3/Subcateg2 which are registered in Category Base are updated.

In Order Management Base, the number of sentences which take an *ORDER* (*A AC P*) increases by 1 to 6.

No new categories are formed in categorization bases.

Because BUD finds that a word *move(AC)z* which is not registered for a concept move is used for the concept, it tries to store *move(AC)z* into Inflection Base as another word for the concept. Because *move* is included in Categ3, BUD searches Categ3 for a unit which has a subcategorical property that suffix [z] can be attached to it. Because Categ3 does not have such a unit, a rule (Categ3/*move* → Categ3/*move*%z) is newly stored there, together with the condition on the application of the rule. This condition is represented as an and/or-tree of depth 0.

Now, BUD compares this condition with that for the application of rule (Categ3/Subcateg2 → Categ3/Subcateg2%iz), because *move* is also a member of Categ3/Subcateg2. Then, the two conditions are completely the same. Therefore, BUD cannot understand which should be used, *move*z or *move*iz, when the condition is satisfied. This violates the assumption that a form is in one-to-one correspondence with a meaning (see Section 4.3). BUD considers that *move*z is correct, and that *move*iz is incorrect, because rule (Categ3/*move* → Categ3/*move*%z) was made more recently than rule (Categ3/Subcateg2 → Categ3/Subcateg2%iz). The word *move* can be regarded as an **implicit negative example** of Categ3/Subcateg2. Every member of Categ3/Subcateg2 has been considered to have both a sub-categorical property that it can take an *ORDER* (*A AC P*), and a sub-categorical property that it can have suffix [iz]. However, BUD has found that *move* ∈ Categ3/Subcateg2 has the former property, but does not have the latter property. Because parameter **disruption-for-sub** = 1, sub-category Categ3/Subcateg2 is disrupted into Categ3/Subcateg0 and Categ3/Subcateg1 (see Section 6.3 (I)). BUD recovers the state shown in Figure 7.14. In this state, Subcateg0 and Subcateg1 have members (95) and members (96), respectively.

(95) Categ3/Subcateg0 = (kiss, open, touch)

(96) Categ3/Subcateg1 = (kiss, touch)

The members of Categ3/Subcateg0 and Categ3/Subcateg1 are the ones existing just before they were integrated into Categ3/Subcateg2 (see Figure 7.7 in Section 7.2.5). Neither of these subcategories have included *move*. An entry for Categ3/Subcateg2 is removed from Category Base, and two entries for Categ3/Subcateg0 and Categ3/Subcateg1 are stored there with their members.

Because BUD can obtain access to the synthetic representation of the ninth sentence (62), the word *move*, which can take an *ORDER* (*A AC P*), becomes a new member of Categ3/Subcateg0. Hence, Categ3/Subcateg0 has had the following members:

(97) Categ3/Subcateg0 = (kiss, move, open, touch)

Accordingly, the members of Categ3/Subcateg2 which are registered in Category Base are updated.

Category Categ3 remembers that a word exists in Categ3 such that it can take an *ORDER* (*A AC P*), but cannot have suffix [iz]. However, Categ3 will not remember which word in Categ3 is problematic.

Expansion Base remains unchanged.

7.3. Values of Parameters

The semantic representation given to BUD in its early stage has a flat structure. That is, the values of its role slots are only simple concepts. Hence, BUD treats a sentence as the one corresponding to one proposition. BUD cannot treat a sentence corresponding to plural propositions as such. Thus, sentences which we use as inputs in the early stage are simple ones, each corresponding to one proposition (see Section 5.2).

BUD has been being implemented in Franz Lisp, Opus 38.92 on a News of Sony. Now, we discuss the values of the six parameters (see Section 7.1), by comparing BUD's behavior in learning English with that of children.

As described in Section 6.1 (I), whether *do-hash-begin* is *t* or *nil*, a category of verbs of adult grammars is easier to make than a category of nouns. A category of nouns is easier to make when *do-hash-begin* is *t* than when it is *nil*. This is because most noun phrases in simple English sentences have nouns as their last words. Determiners and modifiers such as adjectives precede nouns in English noun phrases. Hence, we have concluded that *do-hash-begin* should be *t*.

Parameter *depth* should be 1. We assumed that BUD is never given syntactically incorrect sentences as inputs (see Section 5.1). When we dare to give BUD a few syntactic incorrect sentences, BUD cannot maintain its normal function if *depth* = 0. On the other hand, BUD makes too many possible synthetic representations if *depth* ≥ 2.

We cannot give any definite values to the remaining four parameters, because all of the phenomena introduced in Section 2.2 can be explained whatever values they may have. The smaller *integration−for−sub* and *integration* are, the sooner overgeneralizations occur. On the other hand, the smaller *disruption−for−sub* and *disruption* are, the later BUD recovers from the confusion. In the went-goed-went phenomenon, it takes about a half of a year to shift from one stage to the next. In the acquisition of the correct use of *tell* and *promise*, it takes about a year to shift from one stage to the next. Whatever the four parameters may be, BUD's category-formation/integration/disruption mechanism accounts for the hidden-parts in these phenomena, that is, what makes children shift from one stage to the next stage, and what they are doing in each stage.

CHAPTER 8

ORDER MODE AND PRODUCTION MODE

This chapter presents data flow in Order Mode and Production Mode. In Order Mode, BUD is given a pair comprising a sentence and its intonation, and returns a semantic representation of the sentence. In Production Mode, BUD is given a semantic representation, and returns a pair comprising a sentence which expresses the semantic representation, and the intonation of the sentence.

8.1. Data Flow in Order Mode

In Order Mode, BUD is given a pair comprising a sentence and its intonation, and returns a semantic representation of the sentence. In this mode, BUD learns nothing, and BUD's ability to comprehend a given sentence is tested (see Section 5.1). Figure 8.1 illustrates the data flow in Order Mode. This figure is very similar to Figure 7.9 in Section 7.2.6. Now, we explain the difference between the data flow in Order Mode and the data flow in

144

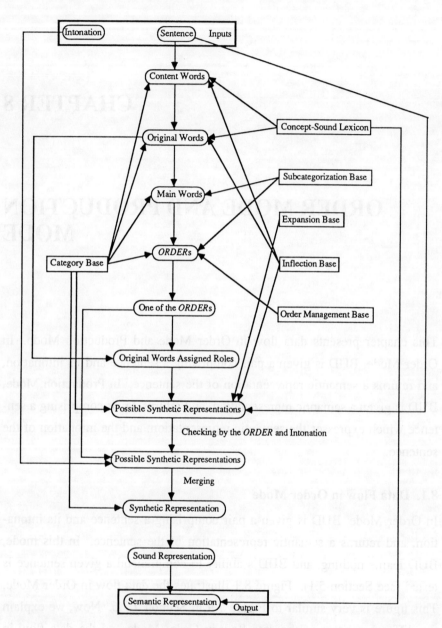

Figure 8.1. Data Flow in Order Mode

making a possible synthetic representation in Learning Mode.

First, in Order Mode, content words are defined as words registered for concepts in Concept-Sound Lexicon or Inflection Base, or words which have the words registered for concepts in Concept-Sound Lexicon, as their root parts.

Second, if BUD cannot find content words which can be main words of sentences, or if BUD cannot analyze a sentence on the basis of any *ORDER*s registered for such words in Subcategorization Base, BUD fetches the top three *ORDER*s stored in Order Management Base, and then tries to analyze a sentence on the basis of the *ORDER* s.

Third, BUD computes a sound representation from a synthetic representation, and then consults Concept-Sound Lexicon, and makes a semantic representation by replacing the sounds as the values of the role slots in the sound representation with concepts corresponding to the sounds.

For example, assume that, as shown in Figure 8.2, BUD is given a pair comprising a sentence (98) and its intonation, after getting the nine sentences in Section 7.2 from the initial state.

(98) The boy kick*s* the girl.

The current state is illustrated by Figure 7.14 in Section 7.2.9. BUD searches the sentence for content words. Then, BUD finds three words, i.e., *boy*, *kicks*, and *girl*. Two words *boy* and *girl* are registered in Concept-Sound Lexicon, and the word *kicks* has *kick* which is registered for concept kick in Concept-Sound Lexicon, as its root part. Note that *kicks* is not registered in Inflection Base. Then, BUD gets the root part of *kicks*, i.e., *kick*. Next, BUD searches these three words, i.e., *boy*, *kick*, and *girl*, for ones registered in Subcategorization Base as words which can be main words of sentences. Then, BUD cannot find such words. Hence, BUD fetches the *ORDER* stored at the top of Order Management Base, and gets

146

Sentence (Input): The boy kicks the girl.

Intonation (Input): ↓

Four Possible Synthetic Representations:

ORDER: —
A: the boy(A)
AC: Categ3
INTONATION: ↑
MOOD: interrogative
TIME: now

(i)

ORDER: A AC P
A: the boy(A)
P: the Categ7
AC: Categ3
INTONATION: ↓
MOOD: declarative
TIME: now

(ii)

ORDER: does A AC P
A: the Categ7
P: the girl(P)
AC: Categ3
INTONATION: ↑
MOOD: interrogative
TIME: now

(iii)

ORDER: A AC P
A: the Categ7
P: the girl(P)
AC: Categ3
INTONATION: ↓
MOOD: declarative
TIME: now

(iv)

Possible synthetic representations (ii) and (iv) are merged into (v).

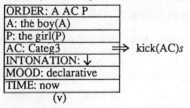

ORDER: A AC P
A: the boy(A)
P: the girl(P)
AC: Categ3
INTONATION: ↓
MOOD: declarative
TIME: now

(v)   ⟹ kick(AC)s

Synthetic Representation:

ORDER: A AC P
A: the boy(A)
P: the girl(P)
AC: kick(AC)s
INTONATION: ↓
MOOD: declarative
TIME: now

(v)

Sound Representation:

A: boy
P: girl
AC: kick
MOOD: declarative
TIME: now

Semantic Representation (Output):

A: boy
P: girl
AC: kick
MOOD: declarative
TIME: now

Figure 8.2. An Example of BUD's Behavior in Order Mode

an *ORDER* (*A AC P*). Because the three words appear in the sentence in the order of *boy*, *kick*, and *girl*, BUD considers that *A*, *AC*, and *P* in the *ORDER* correspond to *boy*, *kick*, and *girl*, respectively.

As shown in Figure 7.14, Expansion Base has an entry for *boy*(*A*) ∈ Categ7 and an entry for *girl*(*P*) ∈ Categ7.

BUD tries to apply rule (Categ7 → the Categ7) stored in Expansion Base to *boy*(*A*). Then, *the boy*(*A*) is made. In fact, the sentence involves *the boy*. As shown in Figure 7.14, the condition on which Categ7 accompanies *the* in *A* phrases is represented as an and/or-tree of depth 1. Thus, two possible synthetic representations (i) and (ii) are made as shown in Figure 8.2.

Next, BUD tries to apply rule (Categ7 → the Categ7) stored in Expansion Base to *girl*(*P*). Then, *the girl*(*P*) is made. In fact, the sentence involves *the girl*. As shown in Figure 7.14, the condition on which Categ7 accompanies *the* in *P* phrases is represented as an and/or-tree of depth 1. Thus, two possible synthetic representations (iii) and (iv) are made as shown in Figure 8.2.

Now, four possible synthetic representations have been made. BUD searches them for ones which satisfy the following two conditions:

- The value of the *ORDER* slot in a possible synthetic representation must match the *ORDER* (*A AC P*).
- The value of the *INTONATION* slot in a possible synthetic representation must match the intonation given with the sentence as an input, i.e., ↓.

Then, (ii) and (iv) satisfy the above conditions. The remaining possible synthetic representations, i.e., (i) and (iii), are discarded.

Next, in (ii), which was made on the basis of the condition on which Categ7 accompanies *the* in *A* phrases, BUD searches all the role slots except the *A* slot for ones whose values are constituted by more than one word. Then, BUD finds the *P* slot. Because the value of the *P* slot in (ii) is *the* Categ7, and because (iv) was made on the basis of the condition on which Categ7 accompanies *the* in *P* phrases, BUD tries to merge (ii) and (iv) into (v).

First, (ii) and (iv) have a common value for each of the *ORDER*, the *AC*, the *INTONATION*, the *MOOD*, and the *TIME* slots. Hence, the values of these five slots in (v) are determined as those values.

Second, by comparing the values of the *A* slots in (ii) and (iv), BUD examines whether or not Categ7 contains *boy*(*A*). Because Categ7 contains *boy*(*A*), the value of the *A* slot in (v) is determined as *the boy*(*A*).

Finally, by comparing the values of the *P* slots in (ii) and (iv), BUD examines whether or not Categ7 contains *girl*(*P*). Because Categ7 contains *girl*(*P*), the value of the *P* slot in (v) is determined as *the girl*(*P*).

Thus, BUD has succeeded in merging (ii) and (iv) into (v). Hence, (ii) and (iv) are discarded.

Now, BUD replaces each role name involved by the value of the *ORDER* slot in (v) with the value of the corresponding role slot in (v), and obtains a sequence of words (the boy(*A*) Categ3 the girl(*P*)). By comparing the resulting sequence of words with sentence (98), BUD infers that an original word *kick* of *kick*s should be a member of Categ3. Then, BUD replaces Categ3 in the value of the *AC* slot in (v) with *kick*(*AC*)s. Because resulting possible synthetic representation (v) does not have any indefinite parts, it is determined as a synthetic representation of sentence (98).

Next, BUD computes a sound representation from the synthetic representation. For example, the value of the *AC* slot in the sound representation is a word followed by (*AC*) in the value of that slot in the synthetic representation. Finally, BUD consults Concept-Sound Lexicon, and makes a semantic representation by replacing the sounds which are the values of the role slots in the sound representation with concepts corresponding to the sounds. BUD returns the semantic representation as an output.

There are some sentences such as (98) which BUD cannot analyze with the knowledge already acquired in Learning Mode, but can analyze in Order Mode. Because BUD learns nothing in Order Mode, BUD tries to comprehend a given sentence positively or somewhat rudely.

If BUD cannot analyze a sentence in Order Mode, it returns only pairs comprising content words which BUD found in the sentence and the concepts corresponding to the content words.

8.2. Data Flow in Production Mode

In Production Mode, BUD is given a semantic representation as an input, and returns a pair comprising a sentence which expresses the semantic representation, and the intonation of the sentence. In this mode, if a sentence or its intonation which BUD returns as an output is not corrected by us, that is, a teacher, BUD learns nothing, and BUD's ability to generate a pair comprising a sentence which expresses a given semantic representation, and the intonation of the sentence is tested (see Section 5.1). Figure 8.3 illustrates the data flow in Production Mode. This figure is very similar to Figure 7.13 in Section 7.2.8. Now, we explain the difference between the data flow in Production Mode and the data flow in learning the meaning of an unknown word in Learning Mode.

First, because BUD is not given an intonation in Production Mode, BUD cannot use it to check possible synthetic representations, which BUD makes by applying the rules stored in Expansion Base or Inflection Base.

Second, if a synthetic representation which BUD makes by merging possible synthetic representations has some indefinite parts in the values of

150

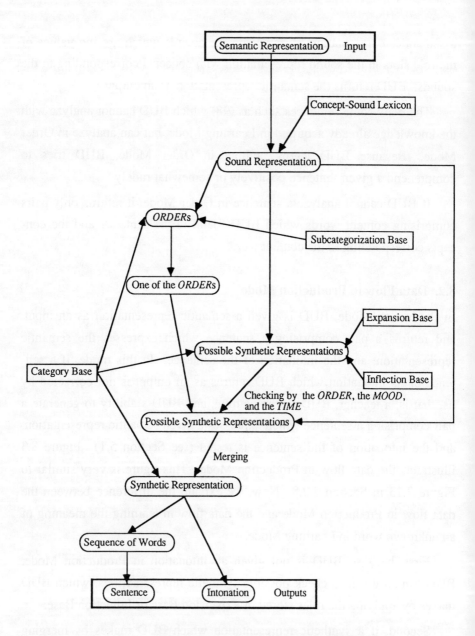

Figure 8.3. Data Flow in Production Mode

its role slots, i.e., wild cards or categories, counterparts of the indefinite parts are missing from a sentence which BUD returns as an output. If the *INTONATION* slot in the synthetic representation has a wild card as its value, the intonation which BUD returns as an output is also a wild card. If a sentence BUD returns as an output is corrected by the teacher, that is, a correct sentence is given to BUD, BUD detects the difference between the correct and the incorrect sentences, and invokes disruption of categories or subcategories (see Section 6.3). The incorrect sentence can be regarded as an explicit negative example.

For example, assume that, as shown in Figure 8.4, BUD is given a semantic representation as an input, after getting the first eight sentences in Section 7.2 from the initial state. The current state is illustrated by Figure 7.12 in Section 7.2.8. Now, a sound representation is computed from the semantic representation and Concept-Sound Lexicon. Note that the *P* slot of the sound representation has a wild card as its value, because Concept-Sound Lexicon does not have an entry for the concept window. A synthetic representation is computed from the sound representation and the information stored in the several databases.

BUD fetches subcategorization information of *open* ∈ Categ3/Subcateg2 from Subcategorization Base, and gets an *ORDER* (*A AC P*). The set of role names (slots) contained in the sound representation must be the same as the set of role names contained in the *ORDER*. Then, they are the same. If this condition were not satisfied, BUD would not be able to generate a sentence which expresses the semantic representation. In such a case, BUD would return only pairs comprising the concepts which are the values of the role slots in the semantic representation and the words registered for the concepts in Concept-Sound Lexicon.

As shown in Figure 7.12, Inflection Base has an entry for *open*(*AC*), and Expansion Base has an entry for *boy*(*A*) ∈ Categ7.

152

The Current State:
See Figure 7.12 in Section 7.2.8.

Semantic Representation (Input):   Sound Representation:

A: boy
P: window
AC: open
MOOD: declarative
TIME: now

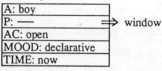

A: boy
P: —
AC: open
MOOD: declarative
TIME: now

⟹ window

Three Possible Synthetic Representations:

ORDER: A AC P
A: the Categ7
P: the Categ7
AC: open(AC)iz
INTONATION: ↓
MOOD: declarative
TIME: now
(i)

ORDER: —
A: the boy(A)
AC: Categ3
INTONATION: ↑
MOOD: interrogative
TIME: now
(ii)

ORDER: A AC P
A: the boy(A)
P: the Categ7
AC: Categ3
INTONATION: ↓
MOOD: declarative
TIME: now
(iii)

Possible synthetic representations (i) and (iii) are merged into a synthetic representation (iv).

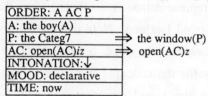

ORDER: A AC P
A: the boy(A)
P: the Categ7
AC: open(AC)iz
INTONATION:↓
MOOD: declarative
TIME: now

⟹ the window(P)
⟹ open(AC)z

Sequence of Words: (the boy open(AC)iz the Categ7)

Sentence (Output): The boy openiz the.

Intonation (Output): ↓

Correct Sentence: The boy open$z$ the window.

Figure 8.4. An Example of BUD's Behavior in Production Mode

Subcategorization Base:
 Categ3 = (go, kiss, open, touch)
 Categ3/go - A AC G
 Categ3/touch - does A AC P
 Categ3/Subcateg2 = (kiss, open, touch)
 Categ3/Subcateg2 - A AC P
 Categ3/Subcateg0 = (kiss, open, touch)
 Categ3/Subcateg0 - A AC P

Order Management Base:
 A AC P - 6
 does A AC P - 2
 A AC G - 1

Inflection Base:
 Categ3/Subcateg2 -> Categ3/Subcateg2%iz
 Categ3/Subcateg1 -> Categ3/Subcateg1%iz
 Categ3's domain is Subcategorization
 Base and AC.

| ORDER: A AC P |
| A: the Categ7 |
| P: the Categ7 |
| INTONATION: ↓ |
| MOOD: declarative |
| TIME: now |

 Categ3/touch -> Categ3/touch%
 Categ3's domain is Subcategorization
 Base and AC.

| ORDER: does A AC P |
| A: the Categ7 |
| P: the Categ7 |
| INTONATION: ↑ |
| MOOD: interrogative |
| TIME: now |

 Categ3/open -> Categ3/open%z
 Categ3's domain is Subcategorization
 Base and AC.

| ORDER: A AC P |
| A: the Categ7 |
| P: the Categ7 |
| INTONATION: ↓ |
| MOOD: declarative |
| TIME: now |

Expansion Base:
 Categ7 -> the Categ7
 Categ7's domain is A and P.
 for A,

| AC: Categ3 |
| TIME: now |

INTONATION: ↑	ORDER: A AC P
MOOD: interrogative	P: the Categ7
	INTONATION: ↓
	MOOD: declarative

 for P,

| A: the Categ7 |
| AC: Categ3 |
| TIME: now |

ORDER: does A AC P	ORDER: A AC P
INTONATION: ↑	INTONATION: ↓
MOOD: interrogative	MOOD: declarative

 kitchen(G) -> to the kitchen(G)

| ORDER: does A AC G |
| A: the Categ7 |
| AC: Categ3 |
| INTONATION: ↑ |
| MOOD: interrogative |
| TIME: now |

Category Base:
 Categ3 = (go, kiss, open, touch)
  Categ3's domain is Subcategorization Base and AC.
 ✓ Categ3/Subcateg2 = (kiss, open, touch)
  Categ3/Subcateg2 is disrupted into
  Categ3/Subcateg0 and Categ3/Subcateg1.
 Categ3/Subcateg0 = (kiss, open, touch)
 Categ3/Subcateg1 = (kiss, touch)
 Categ7 = (boy, cat, door, father, girl, mother, window)
  Categ7's domain is A and P.

Concept-Sound Lexicon
 See Section 7.2.
 cat - cat
 window - window

Figure 8.4. An Example of BUD's Behavior in Production Mode (Continued)

154

Categorization Bases
A Categorization Base:

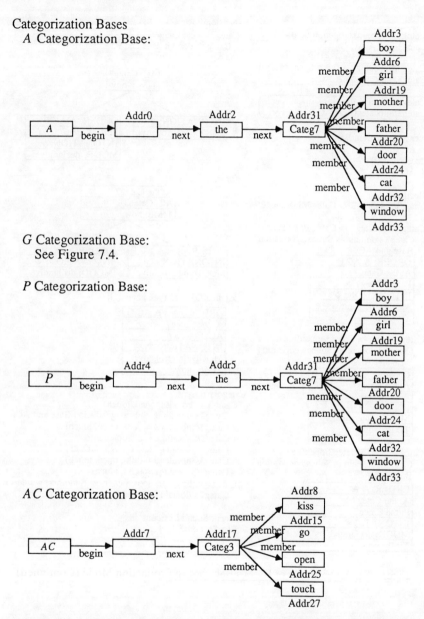

G Categorization Base:
See Figure 7.4.

P Categorization Base:

AC Categorization Base:

Figure 8.4. An Example of BUD's Behavior in Production Mode (Continued)

BUD tries to apply rule (Categ3/Subcateg2 → Categ3/Subcateg2%iz) stored in Inflection Base to *open(AC)*. Then, *open(AC)*iz is made. As shown in Figure 7.12, the condition on the application of the rule is represented as an and/or-tree of depth 0. Thus, a possible synthetic representation (i) is made as shown in Figure 8.4.

Next, BUD tries to apply rule (Categ7 → the Categ7) stored in Expansion Base to *boy(A)*. Then, *the boy(A)* is made. As shown in Figure 7.12, the condition on the application of the rule is represented as an and/or-tree of depth 1. Thus, two possible synthetic representations (ii) and (iii) are made as shown in Figure 8.4.

Now, three possible synthetic representations have been made. BUD searches them for ones which satisfy the following three conditions:

- The value of the *ORDER* slot in a possible synthetic representation must match the *ORDER* (*A AC P*).
- The value of the *MOOD* slot in a possible synthetic representation must match the value of that slot in the sound representation.
- The value of the *TIME* slot in a possible synthetic representation must match the value of that slot in the sound representation.

Then, (i) and (iii) satisfy the above conditions. The remaining possible synthetic representation, i.e., (ii), is discarded. Note that BUD cannot check possible synthetic representations by an intonation, because it is not given to BUD as an input in Production Mode.

Next, in (i), which was made on the basis of the condition on the application of rule (Categ3/Subcateg2 → Categ3/Subcateg2%iz), BUD searches the role slots for ones whose values are constituted by more than one word. Then, BUD finds the *A* and the *P* slots, both of which have *the* Categ7 as their values. Because (iii) was made on the basis of the condition on which Categ7 accompanies *the* in *A* phrases, BUD tries to merge (i) and (iii) into (iv).

First, (i) and (iii) have a common value for each of the *ORDER*, the *P*, the *INTONATION*, the *MOOD*, and the *TIME* slots. Hence, the values of the five slots in (iv) are determined as those values.

Second, by comparing the values of the *A* slots in (i) and (iii), BUD examines whether or not Categ7 contains *boy*(*A*). Because Categ7 contains *boy*(*A*), the value of the *A* slot in (iv) is determined as *the boy*(*A*).

Finally, by comparing the values of the *AC* slots in (i) and (iii), BUD examines whether or not Categ3 contains *open*(*AC*). Because Categ3 contains *open*(*AC*), the value of the *AC* slot in (iv) is determined as *open*(*AC*)*iz*.

Thus, BUD has succeeded in merging (i) and (iii) into (iv). Hence, (i) and (iii) are discarded. Although (iv) has an indefinite part in the value of the *P* slot, it is determined as a synthetic representation of a sentence which BUD will return as an output.

Now, BUD replaces each role name involved by the value of the *ORDER* slot in the synthetic representation with the value of the corresponding role slot in the synthetic representation, and obtains a sequence of words (the boy(*A*) open(*AC*)*iz* the Categ7). Finally, BUD returns a pair comprising a sentence and its intonation as shown in Figure 8.4.

Furthermore, assume that a teacher gives a correct sentence (99) to BUD.

(99) The boy open*z* the window.

Then, by comparing the sequence of words with (99), BUD infers that *window* should be a member of Categ7. BUD replaces Categ7 in the value of the *P* slot in the synthetic representation with *window*(*P*). Next, the wild card in the *P* slot of the sound representation is replaced with *window*. By comparing the values of the *P* slots in the sound representation and the semantic representation, BUD determines the sound corresponding to concept window as *window*. Then, a new pair comprising concept window and sound *window* is registered in Concept-Sound Lexicon. In this way, BUD may learn sounds corresponding to concepts which are values of role slots in a given semantic representation by receiving a correct sentence.

By comparing the correct sentence with the sequence of words, BUD has found that *open* does not have suffix [iz], but has suffix [z]. Then, BUD replaces *open(AC)iz* in the value of the *AC* slot in the synthetic representation with *open(AC)z*. The word *open* can be regarded as an explicit negative example of Categ3/Subcateg2. Every member of Categ3/Subcateg2 has been considered to have both a subcategorical property that it can take an *ORDER* (*A AC P*), and a subcategorical property that it can have suffix [iz]. However, BUD has found that *open* ∈ Categ3/Subcateg2 has the former property, but does not have the latter property. Because parameter *disruption-for-sub* = 1, subcategory Categ3/Subcateg2 is disrupted into Categ3/Subcateg0 and Categ3/Subcateg1 (see Section 6.3 (I)). BUD recovers the state shown in Figure 8.4. In this state, Subcateg0 and Subcateg1 have members (95) and members (96), respectively.

(95) Categ3/Subcateg0 = (kiss, open, touch)

(96) Categ3/Subcateg1 = (kiss, touch)

The members of Categ3/Subcateg0 and Categ3/Subcateg1 are the ones existing just before they were integrated into Categ3/Subcateg2 (see Figure 7.7 in Section 7.2.5). An entry for Categ3/Subcateg2 is removed from Category Base, and the entries for Categ3/Subcateg0 and Categ3/Subcateg1 are stored there with their members.

Although BUD can obtain access to the synthetic representation of sentence (99), the members of Categ3/Subcateg0 remain unchanged, because the word *open* which can take an *ORDER* (*A AC P*) has already been a member of Categ3/Subcateg0.

When a correct sentence is given to BUD, BUD learns the syntax of the language being learned, meanings of unknown words, inflections of words, and so on in Production Mode as well as in Learning Mode.

In Order Management Base, the number of sentences which take an *ORDER* (*A AC P*) increases by 1 to 6.

No new categories are formed in categorization bases.

Because BUD finds that the word *open*(*AC*)z, which is not registered for a concept open, is used for the concept, it tries to store *open*(*AC*)z into Inflection Base as another word for the concept. Because *open* is included in Categ3, BUD searches Categ3 for a unit which has a subcategorical property that suffix [z] can be attached to it. Because Categ3 does not have such a unit, a rule (Categ3/*open* → Categ3/*open*%z) is newly stored there with the condition on the application of the rule. This condition is represented as an and/or-tree of depth 0.

Expansion Base remains unchanged.

CHAPTER 9

FINAL REMARKS

9.1. Conclusions

We have developed a model named BUD (*B*ring *U*p a *D*aughter) of first
language acquisition on the basis of the following matters:

- common stages children pass through (see Section 2.1)

- overgeneralizations as common errors made by children (see Section
  2.2)

- the primary data given to them as inputs (see Section 2.3 and Section
  2.4)

- Gold's theory about learnability of classes of formal languages (see
  Chapter 3)

BUD is based on the empiricists' view (see Section 1.2). That is, it has no
built-in knowledge about language structures, but has a built-in procedure
by which it computes the structure of a given language.

Children are positive learners of languages they first meet. Once they form a rule or a principle, they tend to apply it to cases to which it should not be applied. This phenomenon is called an overgeneralization. First language acquisition can be regarded as learning the correct application of a number of rules through overgeneralizations. Although several overgeneralizations have been reported, existing models deal with them separately.

Properties of words can be divided into two types, i.e., categorical properties and subcategorical properties (see Section 6.1 (IV)). When BUD finds that two or more words have a common categorical property, it forms a category. A category may have subcategories. When it finds that two or more words in a category have a common subcategorical property, it forms a subcategory of this category. Thus, categories have two-level structures. A rule can be regarded as a categorical or subcategorical property which words have in common. Although we have restricted a rule to the one related to words, we believe that almost all of the phenomena of overgeneralizations can be explained. This is guaranteed by recent linguistic theories such as the GB theory and HPSG (see Section 2.2).

In the databases, BUD forms rules, and learns their correct application concurrently. BUD accounts for overgeneralizations of rules as the results of interactions among rule-learning processes. The data flow among databases in Learning Mode, which is illustrated by Figure 5.1 in Section 5.1, is designed so that the relationship between categories and their subcategories can be preserved, and that the processes for learning rules can interact with one another. BUD deals with such interactions by its category-formation/integration/disruption mechanism. On the basis of this mechanism, we made some predictions about the hidden parts in the went-goed-went phenomenon (see Section 6.4).

As we introduced in Section 2.2, overgeneralizations can be found in the acquisition of every aspect of a language. They are strong evidence which supports the empiricists' view. If children were passive learners of languages, such overgeneralizations would never occur.

9.2. Future Work

As future work, we envisage the following three tasks:

(I) Nondeterministic Behavior

In the current system, how the internal state changes by getting an input sentence is precisely determined. For example, which categories are formed, or which categories are disrupted is precisely determined. However, it is hard to imagine that children have such a deterministic and accurate mechanism. They may make some errors, or the values of parameters may change case by case. Therefore, we have to develop a mechanism for BUD to behave itself nondeterministically.

(II) Introducing a One-Dimensional Semantic Representation into BUD

This monograph has presented BUD's behavior in its early stage. In this stage, a semantic representation which BUD is given as an input or returns as an output has a flat structure, so that BUD treats a sentence as one corresponding to one proposition (see Section 5.2). BUD cannot treat a sentence corresponding to plural propositions as such. For example, a sentence which has a noun phrase containing a relative clause, or a sentence which has a subordinate clause corresponds to plural propositions. Even a sentence which has a noun phrase containing an adjective as a modifier of its head corresponds to plural propositions.

We plan to introduce a one-dimensional semantic representation into BUD as a new temporal representation so that we can present BUD's behavior in its late stage in which it deals with a sentence corresponding to plural propositions as such. For example, assume that, as shown in Figure 9.1, the meaning of sentence (100) which corresponds to five propositions is

Sentence: The boy who was clever caught the dirty cockroach the rat the cat chase*t* saw.

Intonation: ↓

Propositional Representations:

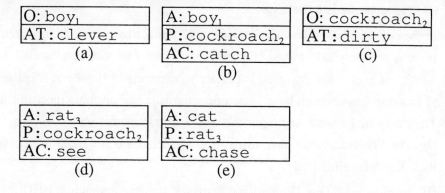

(a)
```
O: boy₁
AT: clever
```

(b)
```
A: boy₁
P: cockroach₂
AC: catch
```

(c)
```
O: cockroach₂
AT: dirty
```

(d)
```
A: rat₃
P: cockroach₂
AC: see
```

(e)
```
A: cat
P: rat₃
AC: chase
```

Figure 9.1. New Representations for BUD's Late Stage

One-Dimensional Semantic Representations:

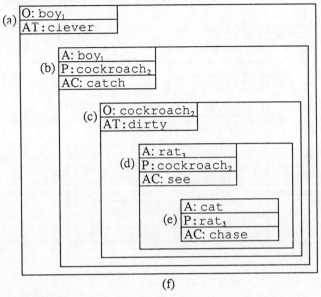

(f)

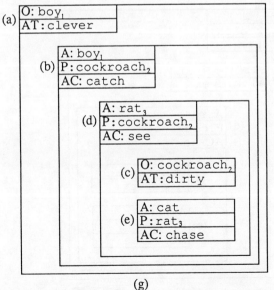

(g)

Figure 9.1. New Representations for BUD's Late Stage (Continued)

164

One-Dimensional Semantic Representations:

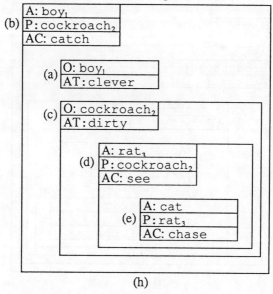

(h)

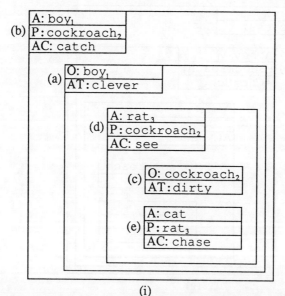

(i)

Figure 9.1. New Representations for BUD's Late Stage (Continued)

One-Dimensional Semantic Representations:

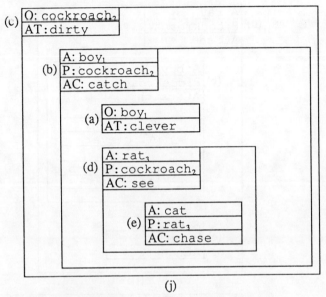

(j)

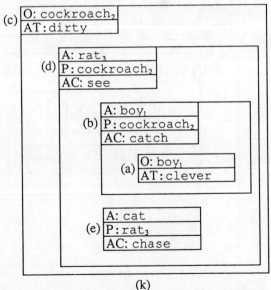

(k)

Figure 9.1. New Representations for BUD's Late Stage (Continued)

166

One-Dimensional Semantic Representations:

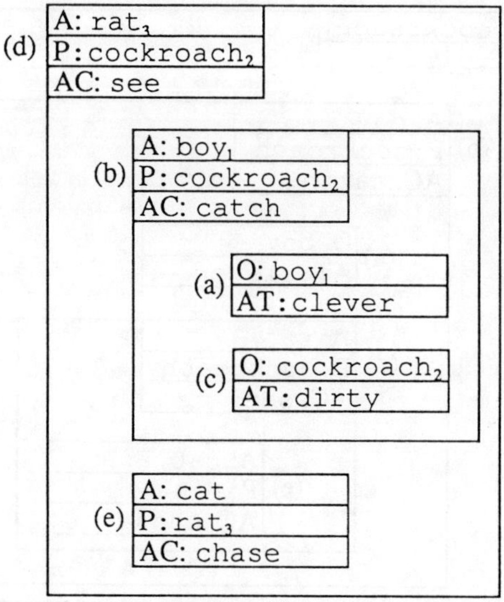

(d)
```
A: rat₃
P: cockroach₂
AC: see
```

(b)
```
A: boy₁
P: cockroach₂
AC: catch
```

(a)
```
O: boy₁
AT: clever
```

(c)
```
O: cockroach₂
AT: dirty
```

(e)
```
A: cat
P: rat₃
AC: chase
```

(l)

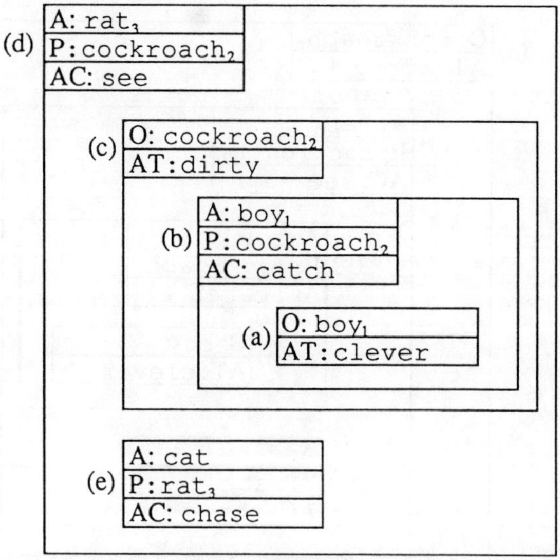

(d)
```
A: rat₃
P: cockroach₂
AC: see
```

(c)
```
O: cockroach₂
AT: dirty
```

(b)
```
A: boy₁
P: cockroach₂
AC: catch
```

(a)
```
O: boy₁
AT: clever
```

(e)
```
A: cat
P: rat₃
AC: chase
```

(m)

Figure 9.1. New Representations for BUD's Late Stage (Continued)

One-Dimensional Semantic Representations:

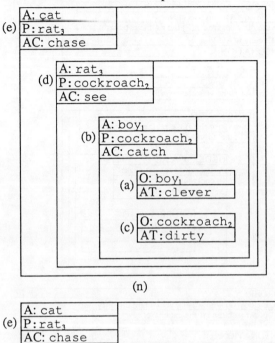

(n)

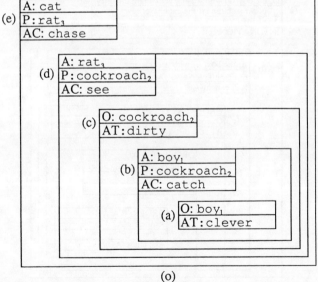

(o)

Figure 9.1. New Representations for BUD's Late Stage (Continued)

168

Synthetic Representations:

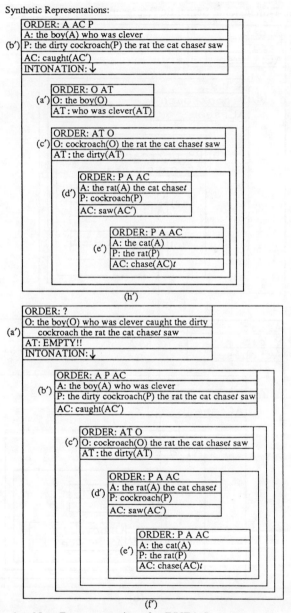

Figure 9.1. New Representations for BUD's Late Stage (Continued)

represented as a set of the five propositional representations, each corresponding to one of the propositions.

(100)The boy who was clever caught the dirty cockroach the rat the cat chase*t* saw.

In (a) and (c), role names O and AT signify an object and an attribute, respectively. We have omitted two pairs of slots and their values, i.e., (*MOOD*: declarative) and (*TIME*: past), from each of the five propositional representations. Concepts which have the same index refer to the same object. For example, *cockroach*es which are the values in the P slot in (b), in the O slot in (c), and in the P slot in (d) have the same index, i.e., 2. Hence, they refer to the same object.

So that a single sentence with no coordinate conjunctions can express five propositions, it must have a hierarchical structure. By combining the five propositional representations, BUD will obtain ten one-dimensional semantic representations, as shown in Figure 9.1, where the two pairs of the slots and their values are also omitted from each propositional representation involved by every one-dimensional semantic representation. A one-dimensional semantic representation has a hierarchical structure, and its format is very similar to that of the Discourse Representation which was originally introduced by Kamp (1981) and is also used by Roberts (1987). A one-dimensional semantic representation is designed so that its correspondence with the sentence is easy to understand.

Now, we explain how to make a one-dimensional semantic representation from propositional representations. Let A be a set of propositional representations.

Step 1. Select one propositional representation PR_1 from A, and remove it from A. Make a box B_1 for PR_1.

Step 2. For each value which has some index in a role slot of PR_1, select one propositional representation PR_2 from A which has a value whose index is the same as its index in some role slot, if any. Remove PR_2 from A. Make a box B_2 for PR_2, and put B_2 in B_1. Let the index be k. We call B_2 a **k-indexed immediately subordinate box** of B_1.

Step 3. Consider P_2 as P_1, and perform Step 2 again.

For a one-dimensional semantic representation to match a sentence, the following three conditions must be satisfied:

(i) Every box must correspond to a group of words in the sentence. No word in the group may be separate from the group.

(ii) The value of each role slot in every propositional representation involved by the one-dimensional semantic representation must correspond to a group of words in the sentence. No word in the group may be separate from the group. If there are no words in the sentence to which it corresponds, the one-dimensional semantic representation does not match the sentence.

(iii) For each value which has some index in a role slot of a propositional representation, check the following: Let the index be k. Then, if the box to which the propositional representation belongs has a k-indexed immediately subordinate box, the group of words in the sentence to which the value corresponds must be the same as the group of words in the sentence to which the k-indexed immediately subordinate box corresponds.

Only one-dimensional semantic representation (h) matches sentence (100). BUD consults Concept-Sound Lexicon, and makes a sound representation by replacing the concepts which are the values of the role slots in each propositional representation involved by the one-dimensional semantic representation with sounds corresponding to the concepts. When the intonation of (100) is ↓, a synthetic representation (h′) of (100) is made as shown in Figure 9.1. We have also omitted two pairs of the slots and their values, i.e., (*MOOD*: declarative) and (*TIME*: past), from the counterpart of each propositional representation in the synthetic representation. Words followed by (AC′) in values of role slots in the synthetic representation indicate that they are irregular words.

For example, the reason why one-dimensional semantic representation (f) does not match sentence (100) is as follows. For (b′) in synthetic representation (f′) to satisfy condition (i), the *A* or *AC* slot of (b′) must include *who was clever*. If neither of these slots included *who was clever*, the words, i.e., *the boy*(*A*), which are the value of the *A* slot would be separate both from the words, i.e., *the dirty cockroach*(*P*) *the rat the cat chase*t *saw*, which are the value of the *P* slot and from the word, i.e., *caught*(*AC′*), which is the value of the *AC* slot. If either of them includes *the boy*(*A*), according to (iii), the value of the *O* slot in (a′) must be the whole sentence. Hence, the *AT* slot in (a′) should be empty. According to (ii), (f) does not match (100).

In the late stage, BUD is given a sentence, its intonation, and a set of propositional representations as a semantic representation of the sentence in Learning Mode. Then, by combining the propositional representations, BUD makes one-dimensional semantic representations. Next, BUD computes a sound representation from each of the one-dimensional semantic representations and Concept-Sound Lexicon. BUD computes a synthetic representation from the sentence, its intonation, and each of the sound representations. BUD examines whether or not the synthetic representation satisfies the above three conditions. If it satisfies them, the one-dimensional semantic representation from which it is derived matches the sentence.

It is very difficult to make BUD shift automatically from its early stage to its late stage. Assume that, in Learning Mode, BUD is given a sentence, its intonation, and a set of propositional representations as a semantic representation of the sentence even in the early stage. In the early stage, BUD must select one of the propositional representations as the one corresponding to the sentence. In the late stage, BUD must make one-dimensional semantic representations by combining the propositional representations. Thus, we have to design BUD so that it can grow in dealing with a given set of propositional representations.

The representations in the databases for the late stage should be different from the those for the early stage. For example, in the late stage, Sub-categorization Base and Order Management Base should treat the order of roles for a main clause and that for a subordinate clause separately. Thus, we have to design BUD so that the representations of the databases can change from the early stage to the late stage.

After due consideration about the above points, we have to devise a mechanism which makes BUD shift automatically from its early stage to its late stage.

(III) A Semantics-Based Strategy

Assume that we know the meanings of words *apple*, *ate*, and *boy*, but that we do not know the syntax of English at all. Then, if we heard the following sentence:

(101)The apple ate the boy.

we would construe *boy* as an agent of an action *eating*, and *apple* as a patient of *eating*. We adults know that most of the agents of *eating* are living things, and that most of its patients are food. Children of two or three years also misunderstand semantically unlikely actives (Strohrer and Nelson 1974). There should be competition between a syntax-based strategy and a semantics-based strategy in the acquisition of order-based languages such as English. We plan to study such semantic aspects of language acquisition.

9.3. Retrospect

We discuss here the difference between children and we adults, that is, the difference between first language acquisition and second language acquisition.

First, according to Miller and Eimas (1983) and Jusczyk, Shea, and Aslim (1984), a child has an innate ability to recognize voices of any languages, and attunes this ability to his native language. At the same time, he is losing the ability to recognize voices which have patterns which cannot be found in his native language. Hence, in learning a second language, we need to regain the ability which we have lost by training. Unfortunately, BUD does not treat such phonological aspects of language development.

Second, we claim here that our fear of making errors causes our difficulty in acquiring a second language. In general, we learn something by making errors. In learning the correct application of most rules, BUD makes errors called overgeneralizations. Such errors seem to assist a child to learn his first language completely. We want to close this monograph with the aphorism that we should not be afraid of making errors when learning a language.

REFERENCES

Aitchison, J. (1983) *The Articulate Mammal: An Introduction to Psycholinguistics*, 2nd ed., Hutchinson Publishing Group, London, England.

Anderson, J. R. (1977) "Induction of Augmented Transition Networks," *Cognitive Science*, 1: 125-157.

Anderson, J. R. (1981) "A Theory of Language Acquisition Based on General Learning Principles," *Proceedings of the Seventh International Joint Conference on Artificial Intelligence*: 97-103.

Atkinson, M. (1986) "Learnability," in P. Fletcher and M. Garman, *Language Acquisition: Studies in First Language Development*, 2nd ed., pp. 90-108, Cambridge University Press, Cambridge, England.

Baker, C. L. (1979) "Syntactic Theory and the Projection Problem," *Linguistic Inquirely*, 10: 533-582.

Berwick, R. C. (1985) *The Acquisition of Syntactic Knowledge*, The MIT Press, Cambridge, Massachusetts.

Bickerton, D. (1981) *Roots of Language*, Karoma, Ann Arbor, Michigan.

Bickerton, D. (1984) "The Language Bioprogram Hypothesis," *Behavioral and Brain Sciences*, 7: 1-49.

Bloom, L. (1973) *One Word at a Time: The Use of Single Word Utterances before Syntax*, Mouton, The Hague.

Bowerman, M. (1973) *Early Syntactic Development: A Cross-Linguistic Study with Special Reference to Finnish*, Cambridge University Press, Cambridge, England.

Braine, M. D. S. (1963) "The Ontogeny of English Phrase Structure: The First Phase," *Language*, 39: 1-13.

Braine, M. D. S. (1971) "The Acquisition of Languages in Infant and Child," in C. Reed, *The Learning of Language,* pp. 153-186, Appleton-Century-Crofts, New York, New York.

Braine, M. D. S. (1976) *Children's First Word Combination*, Monograph of the Society for Research in Child Development 41 (Serial No. 64).

Brown, R., C. B. Cazden, and U. Bellugi (1967) *The Children's Grammar from I to III*, Paper read at 1967 Minnesota Symposium on Child Psychology, Minneapolis.

Brown, R. (1973) *A First Language: The Early Stages*, Harvard University Press, Cambridge, Massachusetts.

Chomsky, C. (1969) *The Acquisition of Syntax in Children from 5 to 10*, The MIT Press, Cambridge, Massachusetts.

Chomsky, N. (1957) *Syntactic Structures*, Janua Linguarum, Series Minor 4, Mouton, The Hague.

Chomsky, N. (1963) "Formal Properties of Grammars," in R. D. Luce, R. Bush and E. Galanter, *Handbook of Mathematical Psychology,* vol. 2, pp. 323-418, Wiley, New York and London.

Chomsky, N. (1965) *Aspects of the Theory of Syntax*, The MIT Press, Cambridge, Massachusetts.

Chomsky, N. (1980) *Rules and Representations*, Basil Blackwell, Oxford.

Chomsky, N. (1981) *Lectures on Government and Binding*, Foris Publications, Dordrecht, Netherlands.

Chomsky, N. (1982) *Some Concepts and Consequences of the Theory of Government and Binding*, Linguistic Inquiry Monograph 6, The MIT Press, Cambridge, Massachusetts.

Chomsky, N. (1986a) *Barriers*, Linguistic Inquiry Monograph 13, The MIT Press, Cambridge, Massachusetts.

Chomsky, N. (1986b) *Knowledge of Language: Its Nature, Origin, and Use*, Praeger, New York.

Chomsky, N. (1987) *Language in a Psychological Setting*, Sophia Linguistica, Working Papers in Linguistics, No. 22, Sophia University, Tôkyô, Japan.

Clark, H. H. and E. V. Clark (1977) *Psychology and Language*, Harcourt Brace Javanovich Inc., New York, New York.

Ervin-Tripp, S. M. (1973) "Imitation and Structural Change in Children's Language," in C. A. Ferguson and D. I. Slobin, *Studies of Child Language Development*, pp. 391-406, Holt, Reinhart and Winston, New York, New York.

Fillmore, C. (1968) "The Case for Case," in E. Bach and R. T. Harms, *Universals in Linguistic Theory*, pp. 1-90, Holt, Rinehart, and Winston, Chicago.

Fletcher, P. (1985) *A Child's Learning of English*, Blackwell, Oxford, England.

Furrow, D., K. Nelson, and H. Benedict (1979) "Mothers' Speech to Children and Syntactic Development: Some Simple Relationships," *Journal of Child Language*, 6: 423-442.

Furrow, D. and K. Nelson (1986) "A Further Look at the Motherese Hypothesis: A Reply to Gleitman, Newport & Gleitman," *Journal of Child Language*, 13: 163-176.

Gleitman, L. R., E. L. Newport, and H. Gleitman (1984) "The Current Status of the Motherese Hypothesis," *Journal of Child Language Development*, 11: 43-79.

Gold, E. M. (1967) "Language Identification in the Limit," *Information and Control*, 10: 447-474.

Greenfield, P. M. and J. H. Smith (1976) *The Structure of a Communication in Early Language Development*, Academic Press, New York, New York.

Grimes, J. (1975) *The Thread of Discourse*, Mouton, The Hague.

Hirsh-Pasek, K., R. M. Golinkoff, S. M. Braidi, and L. McNalty (1986) "'Daddy Throw' On the Existence of Implicit Negative Evidence for Subcategorization Errors," Paper presented at the 11th Annual Conference on Language Development, October.

Johnston, J. R. (1985) "Cognitive Prerequisites: The Evidence from Children Learning English," in D. I. Slobin, *The Cross Linguistic Study of Language Acquisition, vol. 2: Theoretical Issues*, pp. 961-1004, Lawrence Erlbaum Associates, Hillsdale, New Jersey.

Jusczyk, P. W., S. L. Shea, and R. N. Aslim (1984) "Linguistic Experience and Infant Speech Perception: A Re-Examination of Eilers, Gavin and Oller (1984)," *Journal of Child Language*, 11: 453-466.

Kaplan, R. M. and J. Bresnan (1982) "Lexical-Functional Grammar: A Formal System for Grammatical Representation," in J. Bresnan, *The

Mental Representation of Grammatical Relations, pp. 173-281, The MIT Press, Cambridge, Massachusetts.

Kamp, H. (1981) "A Theory of Truth and Semantic Representation," in J. Groenendijk, T. M. V. Janssen, and M. Stokhof, *Formal Methods in the Study of Language*: Proceedings of the Third Amsterdam Colloquium, March 25-28, 1980, pp. 277-322, Mathematical Centre Tracts 135, Mathematisch Centrum, Amsterdam, Netherlands. Reprinted in Groenendijk, Janssen, and Stokhof (1984), pp. 1-41, *Truth, Interpretation and Information*, Foris Publications, Dordrecht, Netherlands.

Kucera, H. and W. Francis (1967) "Computational Analysis of Present-Day American English," Brown University Press, Providence, Rhode Island.

Langley, P. (1980) "Production System Model of First Language Acquisition," *Proceedings of the Eighth International Conference on Computational Linguistics*: 183-189.

Langley, P. (1982) "Language Acquisition through Error Recovery," *Cognition and Brain Theory*, 5, 211-255.

Langley, P. and J. G. Carbonell (1987) "Language Acquisition and Machine Learning," in B. MacWhinney, *Mechanisms of Language Acquisition*, pp. 115-155, Lawrence Erlbaum Associates, Hillsdale, New Jersey.

McNeill, D. (1970) *The Acquisition of Language: The Study of Developmental Psycholinguistics*. Harper and Row, New York, New York.

Maratsos, M., D. E. C. Fox, J. A. Becker, and M. A. Chalkley (1985) "Semantic Restrictions on Children's Passives," *Cognition*, 19: 167-191.

Miller, J. L., and P. D. Eimas (1983) "Studies on the Categorization of Speech by Infants," *Cognition*, 13: 135-165.

180

Morgan, J. L. (1986) *From Simple Input to Complex Grammar*, The MIT Press, Cambridge, Massachusetts.

Murata, K. (1984) *Nihon no Gengo Hattatsu Kenkyû* (*Studies on Language Development in Japan*, in Japanese), Baihûkan, Tokyô, Japan.

Newport, E. L. (1977) "Motherese: The Speech of Mothers to Young Children," in N. J. Castellan, D. B. Pisoni, and G. R. Potts, *Cognitive Theory*, vol. 2, pp. 177-217, Lawrence Erlbaum Associates, Hillsdale, New Jersey.

Newport, E. L., H. Gleitman, and L. R. Gleitman (1977) "Mother, I'd Rather Do It Myself: Some Effects and Non-effects of Maternal Speech Style," in C. Snow and C. A. Ferguson, *Talking to Children*, pp. 109-149, Cambridge University Press, Cambridge, England.

Piatelli-Palmarini, M. (ed.) (1980) *Language and Learning: The Debate between Jean Piaget and Noam Chomsky*, Harvard University Press, Cambridge, Massachusetts.

Pinker, S. (1982) "A Theory of the Acquisition of Lexical Interpretive Grammars," in J. Bresnan, *The Mental Representation of Grammatical Relations*, pp. 655-726, The MIT Press, Cambridge, Massachusetts.

Pinker, S. (1984) *Language Learnability and Language Development*, Harvard University Press, Cambridge, Massachusetts.

Pinker, S. (1987) "The Bootstrapping Problem in Language Acquisition," in B. MacWhinney, *Mechanisms of Language Acquisition*, pp. 399-441, Lawrence Erlbaum Associates, Hillsdale, New Jersey.

Pollard, C. (1984) "Generalized Phrase Structure Grammars, Head Grammars and Natural Language," *Ph. D. Dissertation*, Stanford University.

Pollard, C. (1985) *Lectures on HPSG*, unpublished manuscript, Stanford University, February.

Pollard, C. and I. A. Sag (1987) *Information-Based Syntax and Semantics, vol. 1: Fundamentals*, CSLI Lecture Notes Number 13.

Roberts, C. (1987) "Modal Subordination, Anaphora, and Distributivity," *Ph. D. Dissertation*, The University of Massachusetts.

Rosenbaum, P. S. (1965) "A Principle Governing Deletion in English Sentential Complementation," *IBM Research Paper*, RC-1519, Yorktown Heights, New York.

Rumelhalt, D. E. and J. L. McClelland (1986) "On Learning the Past Tenses of English Verbs," in J. L. McClelland, D. E. Rumelhalt, and the PDP Research Group, *Parallel Distributed Processing, vol. 2: Psychological and Biological Models*, pp. 216-271, The MIT Press, Cambridge, Massachusetts.

Rumelhalt, D. E. and J. L. McClelland (1987) "Learning the Past Tenses of English Verbs: Implicit Rules or Parallel Distributed Processing?," in B. MacWhinney, *Mechanisms of Language Acquisition*, pp. 195-248, Lawrence Erlbaum Associates, Hillsdale, New Jersey.

Satake, N. (1986) "Machine Translation of Natural Language Including Metaphors," *Master's Thesis*, University of Tokyo.

Satake, N. and H. Yamada (1987) "Machine Translation of Natural Language Expressions Including Metaphors," *Technical Report*, 87-21, University of Tokyo.

(This paper was submitted to *Computational Linguistics*, and is now under revision.)

Schank, R. C. (1972) "Conceptual Dependency: A theory of Natural Language Understanding," *Cognitive Psychology*, 3: 552-631.

Schank, R. C. (1973) "Identification of Conceptualizations Underlying Natural Language," in R. C. Schank and K. M. Colby, *Computer Models of Thought and Language,* Freeman, San Francisco, California.

Selfridge, M. (1981) "A Computer Model of Child Language Learning," *Proceedings of the Seventh International Joint Conference on Artificial Intelligence*: 92-96.

Selfridge, M. (1986) "A Computer Model of Child Language Learning," *Artificial Intelligence*, 29: 171-216.

Shieber, S. M. (1985) "Evidence against the Non-Context-Freeness of Natural Language," *Linguistics and Philosophy*, 8: 333-343.

Slobin, D. I. (1966) "Grammatical Transformations and Sentence Comprehension in Childhood and Adulthood," *Journal of Verbal Learning and Verbal Behavior*, 5: 219-227.

Slobin, D. I. (1971) *Psycholinguistics*, Scott, Foresman and Company, Grenview, Illinois.

Slobin, D. I. (1973) "Cognitive Prerequisites for the Development of Grammar," in C. A. Ferguson and D. I. Slobin, *Studies of Child Language Development*, pp. 175-208, Holt, Reinhart, and Winston, New York, New York.

Slobin, D. I. (1985) "Crosslinguistic Evidence for the Language-Making Capacity," in D. I. Slobin, *The Cross Linguistic Study of Language Acquisition, vol. 2: Theoretical Issues*, pp. 1157-1256, Lawrence Erlbaum Associates, Hillsdale, New Jersey.

Smith, N. V. (1973) *The Acquisition of Phonology: A Case Study*, Cambridge University Press, Cambridge, London.

Snow, C. E. (1977) "Mothers' Speech Research: From Input to Interaction," in C. E. Snow and C. A. Ferguson, *Talking to Children*, pp.

31-49, Cambridge University Press, Cambridge, England.

Strohrer, H. and K. E. Nelson (1974) "The Young Child's Development of Sentence Comprehension: Influence of Event Probability, Nonverbal Context, Syntactic Form, and Strategies," *Child Development*, 45: 567-576.

Sugimoto, T. (1985) "Pijin towa Nanika? Kureôru towa Nanika? (What is a Pidgin? What is a Creole? in Japanese)" Gengo (Language), 14(11): 40-44.

Sutton-Smith, B. (1973) "Child Psychology," Appleton-Century-Crofts, New York, New York.

Wexler, K. and P. W. Culicover (1980) *Formal Principles of Language Acquisition*, The MIT Press, Cambridge, Massachusetts.

Wexler, K. (1986) "Negative Evidence and Learnability," Paper presented at the 11th Annual Conference on Language Development, October.

Winston, P. H. (1975) "Learning Structural Descriptions from Examples," in P. H. Winston, *The Psychology of Computer Vision*, pp. 157-209, McGraw-Hill, New York, New York.

Wolff, J. G. (1982) "Language Acquisition, Data Compression, and Generalization," *Language Communication*, 2: 57-89.

AUTHOR INDEX

SUBJECT INDEX